Twelve Extraordinary Women
Workbook

HOW GOD SHAPED WOMEN *of the* BIBLE, *and* WHAT HE WANTS *to* DO *with* YOU

John MacArthur

THOMAS NELSON
Since 1798

NASHVILLE DALLAS MEXICO CITY RIO DE JANEIRO BEIJING

Published by Nelson Impact, a Division of Thomas Nelson, Inc., P.O. Box 141000, Nashville, Tennessee, 37214.

Published in association with the literary agency of Wolgemuth & Associates, Inc.

All Scripture references are from The New King James Version®. Copyright © 1982 by Thomas Nelson, Inc. Used by permission. All rights reserved.

ISBN-10: 1-4185-0557-9
ISBN-13: 978-1-4185-0557-8

Printed in the United States of America.

06 07 08 09 10 VG 9 8 7 6 5 4 3 2 1

CONTENTS

INTRODUCTION
Ordinary or Extraordinary?

The women chosen for the book *Twelve Extraordinary Women* were genuinely ordinary when it came to their human backgrounds and innate talents. In some cases, they were shockingly low-caste women or women without any particular distinction. But they were made extraordinary through memorable, life-changing encounters with the God of the universe. God used these women for His divine purposes. He refined them like silver and because of the gracious work of God, they stand as reminders to us of both our fallenness and our potential. Speaking together as one, they point us to Christ and exemplify God's Word: "God has chosen the foolish things of the world to put to shame the wise, and God has chosen the weak things of the world to put to shame the things which are mighty; and the base things of the world and the things which are despised God has chosen, and the things which are not, to bring to nothing the things that are, that no flesh should glory in His presence" (1 Cor. 1:27–29).

The message for today is this: as you imitate the faithfulness of these women and learn to love the Savior whose work made them extraordinary, your life also can be extraordinary.

How to Use This Companion
Workbook and Study Guide

This workbook is designed as a companion to *Twelve Extraordinary Women*. You are encouraged to cross-check the Scriptures used in the workbook and book, and to grapple with the passages on which the main teachings are based. The workbook serves as a directed Bible study about twelve women who lived ordinary lives with extraordinary purposes!

You may choose to use this workbook for individual or small-group study in twelve sessions. The lessons call for reflection on the Bible passages and teachings, as well as applications to everyday life.

If you are planning to use this workbook for a group study, you are encouraged to make certain each member of the group has a personal copy of the book *and* the workbook. At the close of each workbook chapter you will find notes and information to assist small-group leaders.

The lessons in the workbook follow this basic format:

READ

READING ASSIGNMENT
—refers to the chapter in the book that is related to the lesson.

BIBLICAL FOCUS
—identifies the key Bible passages associated with or included in the lesson.

REVIEW

ANOTHER LOOK
—provides an opportunity for the reader to review the chapter content in the book.

BIBLE CONNECTIONS

—gives an opportunity to take a direct look at Bible passages covered in the chapter.

HIGHLIGHTING THE LESSON

—these questions reflect upon the central points of each chapter.

LASTING IMPLICATIONS

—allows you to draw conclusions about how the chapter's content relates to your personal life.

REFLECT AND RESPOND

DAILY ASSIGNMENTS
—the material of the chapter is broken down into five units or sets of questions to help you apply the material in the chapter to your daily life. Each assignment includes opportunities for reflection, response, and prayer.

NOTES TO LEADERS

These notes are related to the *ANOTHER LOOK* section of the REVIEW questions. A person doing this study on an individual basis might check his or her responses against these notes. Additional questions are provided to prompt group discussion or to extend personal contemplation.

ADDING TO YOUR UNDERSTANDING

Also in each chapter you will find one or more set-apart segments under the heading "Adding to Your Scriptural Vocabulary and Understanding." These additional comments are not directly linked to the chapter content but do relate to concepts addressed in the chapter. The segments include a question or concept for personal consideration or small-group discussion.

1

EVE: MOTHER OF ALL LIVING

Adam called his wife's name Eve, because she was the mother of all living.

(GEN. 3:20)

READ

READING ASSIGNMENT
Read both the Introduction and Chapter 1 of *Twelve Extraordinary Women.*

BIBLICAL FOCUS
Key passages related to this section of the book: Genesis 2:20–25; Genesis 3:1–21; and Genesis 4:1, 25.

REVIEW

ANOTHER LOOK
The following questions will help you review the material in Chapter 1.

1. If you met Eve on the first day of her creation, and then were asked to describe her to a friend, what descriptive words would you use? Choose several words and elaborate upon them if necessary.

2. What do we *know* about Eve from the Scripture? (List several facts.)

   What *don't* we know about Eve? (List several items.)

3. Identify four main truths we can draw from the way in which Eve was created?

4. What is Satan's *modus operandi* in temptation?

5. In what ways do people today try to cover the shame and guilt brought on by their sins?

6. In what ways did the curses of the serpent and Adam also impact Eve?

7. In which four areas could Eve still take comfort and hope after she had sinned?

BIBLE CONNECTIONS

These questions give you an opportunity to reflect on specific biblical passages associated with this lesson.

1. Read Genesis 2:20–25. In what ways was Eve's creation totally initiated and accomplished by God?

2. Read 1 Corinthians 11:3–9, 14; 14:34–35; and 1 Timothy 2:11–15. Also read Colossians 2:9 and Philippians 2:6. In what ways was woman created to be "subordinate, yet equal"?

3. Read Genesis 3:1–7. Compare to Genesis 2:16–17. In what ways might we be prone to misunderstanding God's commandments just as Eve apparently did?

4. Read Genesis 3:4–5. What four things did Satan promise to Eve if she would eat the fruit God had forbidden?

5. Read Romans 5:12; 1 Timothy 2:14; and Romans 5:18–19. Why was it Adam's failure that was so decisive for humanity, rather than Eve's eating of the forbidden fruit?

6. Read Genesis 3:8–13. What were the three main responses Adam and Eve both had toward their sin?

7. Read James 1:13–14 and 1 Timothy 2:14. Why must we take full responsibility for our own sins?

8. Read Romans 16:20; Hebrews 2:14; 1 John 3:8; and Galatians 4:4. What is the biblical understanding regarding the "crushing" of Satan by Jesus Christ?

HIGHLIGHTING THE LESSON

1. In your own words, how do you explain the biblical principle that Adam and Eve were two persons who were truly equal, and yet had a relationship in which Adam was the head and Eve submitted to him?

2. The curse placed on Eve directly impacted her relationship with her husband and children. How can a woman today live free of that curse?

3. In what ways did the curse against the serpent hold a promise for Eve?

LASTING IMPLICATIONS

1. Why are the issues of headship and submission in the story of Eve so crucial to our understanding of the gospel today, and especially the issue of Christ's headship over the redeemed race?

2. In what ways are we each like Eve—guilty of the same sins and responses to our own sin:

- Disobeying God's commands

- Enticing others to join us in our sin

- Trying to hide from God

• Shifting blame to others

3. In what ways are we still dealing with the curse of sin?

In what ways can we live free of the curse?

REFLECT AND RESPOND

DAILY ASSIGNMENT

Day One—The Perfect Woman

Scripture gives us no physical description of Eve. Her beauty—splendid as it must have been—is never mentioned or even alluded to. The focus of the biblical account is on Eve's duty to her Creator and her role alongside her husband. That is a significant fact, reminding us that the chief distinguishing traits of true feminine excellence are nothing superficial.

1. REFLECT: Review the list of Eve's attributes you developed in your answer to the first question in the section titled *ANOTHER LOOK*.
   Are you describing your concept of the "perfect woman"? What other attributes would you like to add to your description?

REFLECT: In what ways do you believe women today attempt to live up to this standard of perfection?

In what ways are you striving for this standard of perfection?

RESPOND: In what ways do you believe God is challenging you to adjust your concept of feminine excellence?

What are the inner spiritual and relational qualities that you believe God has built into you as the chief distinguishing traits of true feminine excellence?

What traits do you believe God desires for you to increase or further develop in your life?

2. REFLECT: How do you believe a Christian woman should respond to the pressures of our culture to be "perfectly" dressed, with "perfect" makeup, hairstyle, and figure?

RESPOND: What are some ways you are being challenged to adjust your own pursuit of perfectionism or your definition of what it means to be perfect? Be specific.

RESPONDING IN PRAYER

Dear Lord, help me today to live according to Your definitions of what makes a woman acceptable, worthy, and righteous in Your eyes. Help me to withstand the pressures of the world to try to be a "perfect" person according to the world's standards. Help me to trust You to develop within me the spiritual and relationship qualities that You admire! In our Lord Jesus' name. Amen.

DAILY ASSIGNMENT

Day Two—Establishing a Complementary Relationship

Adam lost a rib, but he gained a loving companion, created especially for him by the Giver of every good and perfect gift (James 1:17).

"The woman was made of a rib out of the side of Adam; not made out of his head to rule over him, nor out of his feet to be trampled upon by him, but out of his side to be equal with him, under his arm to be protected, and near his heart to be beloved."
—Matthew Henry.

1. REFLECT: What does it mean to have a complementary relationship between a man and woman?

   REFLECT: Although Eve was of one essence with Adam, his spiritual and intellectual peer, and with equal standing before God, in what ways does the Bible present Eve as having a different role?

RESPOND: What are the most significant challenges you face in seeking to fulfill a complementary role?

2. REFLECT: What types of pressure do you feel, or have you felt, to pursue equality with other people, and—especially if you are a woman—equality with men?

ADDING TO YOUR SCRIPTURAL VOCABULARY AND UNDERSTANDING

BE FRUITFUL AND MULTIPLY; FILL THE EARTH AND SUBDUE IT: After creating the universe, God created His representatives, man and woman, to have dominion over it. They were not only His representatives but His representation, created in His image and likeness. Man and woman equally shared God's image and together exercised dominion over creation. They were by divine design physically diverse in order to accomplish God's mandate to multiply, something neither one could do without the other. The commands to have dominion over creation and to subdue it separated mankind from the rest of living creation. Mankind was to oversee creation's operation. To "subdue" does not suggest a wild and unruly condition for the creation that God had pronounced as "good." Rather, it speaks of a productive ordering of the earth and its inhabitants to yield its riches and accomplish God's purposes.

CONSIDER: In what ways are women to work with men to have dominion over creation and subdue it?

REFLECT: How have you competed with another person in an effort to gain equality with that person? Be specific.

RESPOND: In what ways might you seek to strengthen a *complementary* relationship with someone with whom you might have been competing for equality?

RESPONDING IN PRAYER

Jesus, I am trusting You today to show me ways in which I might develop a "complementary" relationship with my husband. Help me to give up my tendencies to compete or to seek independent equality. Free me, Lord, from feeling that I should live up to the world's definitions for my role as a wife, and to follow instead what Your Word presents as the correct way to relate to my spouse. In our Lord Jesus' name. Amen.

DAILY ASSIGNMENT

Day Three—Spiritual Vulnerability

Satan came to Eve in disguise when she was in the most vulnerable position possible.

1. REFLECT: To what natural desires in Eve was Satan aiming with his "disguise"?

REFLECT: In what ways was Eve in a "vulnerable position"?

REFLECT: Eve very likely knew the commandment of God from what Adam had told her—the commandment was given to Adam before Eve was created. How did she misunderstand the commandment? In what ways can "misunderstanding" put us into a spiritually vulnerable position?

REFLECT: We can easily misunderstand God's instructions if we rely only on what other people tell us. Ideally, every instruction attributed to God should be supported in Scripture. Identify a specific example when you or someone you know failed to verify the authenticity of a second-hand instruction.

RESPOND: How can we best protect ourselves from the vulnerabilities we see in Eve?

2. REFLECT: Read John 8:44. How can a person discern a lie?

RESPOND: Is there a lie that you have "swallowed" that you know you must reject? How might you go about doing this?

RESPONDING IN PRAYER

Heavenly Father, protect me against the lies and deceitful tricks of the enemy. Help me to discern clearly lie from truth. Help me to reject and overturn the lies that I have accepted as truth in the past. In our Lord Jesus' name. Amen.

DAILY ASSIGNMENT

Day Four—The Lie of All Lies

Buried in the middle of those words is the lie of all lies. It is the same falsehood that still feeds the carnal pride of our fallen race and corrupts every human heart. This evil fiction has given birth to every false religion in human history. It is the same error that gave birth to the wickedness of Satan himself. This one lie therefore underlies a whole universe of evil: "You will be like God".

1. REFLECT: Why is it wrong to believe that we can ever "be like God"?

   REFLECT: You are either seeking wisdom or refusing to seek wisdom. Which phrase best describes your day-to-day activities?

   REFLECT: Why is it important to pursue the knowledge of what is "good" without gaining the knowledge of what is "evil"?

   RESPOND: What problem or decision are you facing that you need to stop trying to figure out? Be specific.

2. REFLECT: How easy is it to give in to a tendency to *try* to "be God" in another person's life, especially the lives of your family members?

RESPOND: Is there a situation or relationship in which you need to turn over the full reigns of control to God? In what ways can you do that?

RESPONDING IN PRAYER

Jesus, I need to learn more about how to grow in wisdom without gaining the knowledge of evil. Please show me how to do this. Show me also how to trust You to deal with my family members, and to trust You to impart Your wisdom to them apart from my constant intervention. Free me from my "playing God" tendencies in the lives of others around me. In our Lord Jesus' name. Amen.

DAILY ASSIGNMENT

Day Five—Dealing with Guilt and Shame

Human religion, philanthropy, education, self-betterment, self-esteem, and all other attempts at human goodness ultimately fail to provide adequate camouflage for the disgrace and shame of our fallen state. All the man-made remedies combined are no more effective for removing the dishonor of our sin than our first parents' attempts to conceal their nakedness with fig leaves. That's because masking over shame doesn't really deal with the problem of guilt before God. Worst of all, a full atonement for guilt is far outside the possibility of fallen men and women to provide for themselves.

1. REFLECT: In what ways do we each try to hide our sin from God?

REFLECT: In what ways have you experienced fear or sorrow in the wake of sin?

RESPOND: What sin or sins do you need to *confess?*

2. REFLECT: In what ways did sin change the relationship between Adam and Eve?

    RESPOND: In what ways have you or do you struggle with "chafing under the headship" of someone, or "desiring to gain dominance over someone"?

    In what ways is the Lord challenging your attitudes toward other people?

3. REFLECT: In what ways did the birth of Eve's children—especially Seth— provide her hope of her ultimate redemption?

    RESPOND: In what ways are you trusting God to work in and through *your* children's lives to overpower Satan?

RESPONDING IN PRAYER

Dear Lord, You alone know all the ways in which I have struggled with sin in my life. I confess to You today that I am a sinner in need of Your forgiveness. With a deep awareness that I cannot be my own savior and that Jesus alone is Savior, I ask You today to forgive me of my sins and to set me free from them. I ask You to help me live free of sin in my relationships with my husband and children. I ask this in our Lord Jesus' name. Amen.

2
SARAH: HOPING AGAINST HOPE

By faith Sarah herself also received strength to conceive seed, and she bore a child when she was past the age, because she judged Him faithful who had promised.

(HEB. 11:11)

READ

READING ASSIGNMENT
Read Chapter 2 of *Twelve Extraordinary Women.*

BIBLICAL FOCUS
Key passages related to this section of the book: Genesis 11:30; Genesis 16–18; and Hebrews 11:11.

REVIEW

ANOTHER LOOK
The following questions will help you review the material in Chapter 2.

1. How would you describe Sarah to a friend who had never heard about her or read her story in the Bible? Choose several words and elaborate upon them if necessary.

   Identify a few of Sarah's weaknesses?

   Identify a few of Sarah's strengths?

2. When she was a young woman, Sarai (Sarah) followed her husband and father-in-law to Haran—a move that completely uprooted her from a highly advanced and sophisticated culture. Then, at age sixty-five, her husband was called to a land neither of them had ever seen. What was Sarah's response to leaving Haran for this unknown "land of promise"?

3. From the time she was sixty-five until she died, Sarah lived a nomadic life—moving from place to place and living in tents. This life was in sharp contrast to the urban environment in which she once had lived. Identify at least three things that made a nomadic life bearable for Sarah.

4. Abraham, Sarah, and Hagar were each guilty—in different ways—of sin, and in relation to the conception of Ishmael, they each reaped bitter fruit as a result of their sin. Identify the sin of each person and the fruit that resulted.

- Abraham

- Sarah

- Hagar

5. In what ways were the name changes for Abram and Sarai—to Abraham and Sarah—significant in helping them continue to believe in the fulfillment of God's promises?

BIBLE CONNECTIONS

These questions give you an opportunity to reflect on specific biblical passages associated with this lesson.

1. Read Genesis 17:15. Sarai's name was not changed to Sarah until she was ninety years old. How does age impact a woman's ability or desire to change?

   What is required for change to be embraced by a woman even in her middle-aged or older years?

2. Read Hebrews 11:11. Sarah is one of only two women mentioned among the "heroes of the faith." The Bible says she "judged Him faithful who had promised" (Heb. 11:11). In your own words, describe what that phrase means to you.

   What are the implications of this phrase in light of your past experience and your hopes for the future?

3. Read Genesis 29:23–31; 2 Samuel 5:13; and 1 Kings 11:1–4. Also read Matthew 19:4–5 and 1 Corinthians 7:2. Respond to this statement: "no good has ever come from any violation of the 'one-flesh' principle of monogamy."

4. Read Genesis 16:6–13. In what ways did God extend mercy to Hagar?

5. Read Genesis 17:1. Prior to God changing the names of Abraham and Sarah, why did God reveal Himself to Abraham with a new name—*El Shaddai*, meaning "Almighty God"?

HOPING AGAINST HOPE

6. Read Genesis 21:6. Why do you believe Sarah named her son *Isaac*, which meant "laughter"? What was at the core of the humor Sarah saw in the way God had dealt with her?

7. Read Galatians 4:24–30. What did Paul teach to the Galatians using the examples of Sarah, Isaac, Hagar, and Ishmael?

8. Read 1 Peter 3:4–6. While Abraham is depicted in the New Testament as the spiritual father of all who believe (Rom. 4:9–11 and Gal. 3:7), Sarah is pictured as the spiritual matriarch and the ancient epitome of all faithful women. In your own words, describe the faithfulness of Sarah.

HIGHLIGHTING THE LESSON

1. Sarah spent the majority of her life believing for the fulfillment of a promise that didn't immediately come to pass. What practical things might a person do to bolster and maintain hope over a long period of time?

2. Sarah's story is an example of God doing things His way and in His timing—not necessarily in normal ways or the ways we might seek to engineer. How important is it to trust God to use us, at any age, to reflect His omnipotence and the perfection of His timing?

21

LASTING IMPLICATIONS

1. Sarah was married to a God-fearing man and together they lived as nomads in a pagan society. On two occasions, she found herself in the harems of godless kings. What are the challenges that God-fearing people face today as they are confronted frequently by godless people who are making godless decisions?

2. What do you believe the Lord might be seeking to accomplish through your life that is far beyond anything *you* can accomplish in your own strength or wisdom?

3. Sarah took very bold steps in securing the position of her son Isaac as the promised heir to Abraham. In what ways are we challenged today to preserve the truth of God's Word so that it remains pure and uncompromised?

REFLECT AND RESPOND

DAILY ASSIGNMENT

Day One—Desire and Identity

From the time she became Abraham's wife, Sarah desired one thing above all others, and that was to have children. But she was barren throughout her normal child-bearing years. She was obviously tortured by her childlessness. Every recorded episode of ill temper or strife in her household was related to her frustrations about her own barrenness. It ate at her. She spent years in the grip of frustration and depression because of it.

"Sarai was barren; she had no child" (Gen. 11:30). That one statement sums up everything Scripture has to say about the first sixty-five years of Sarah's life.

1. REFLECT: To a woman whose name means "princess"—and to any woman who might have a "princess complex" and is accustomed to getting everything that she wants out of life—how difficult is it to face personal loss, failure, or a lack of achieving something desperately desired?

   RESPOND: What is something you have wanted all of your life but still have not received?

   How is the Lord challenging you to deal with that unfulfilled desire?

2. REFLECT: In what ways are we prone to seeing ourselves through the lens of what we *don't* have instead of what we *do* have?

   RESPOND: Write several objective sentences describing your life. Example: Linda is fruitful; she has. . .

   Take a look at what you have written. Have you focused on what you desire but don't have, or upon what you have or have accomplished by God's grace?

In what ways might the Lord be challenging you to change your perspective on your own life?

In what ways might the Lord be challenging you to seek a new "description" for your life in the days ahead?

ADDING TO YOUR SCRIPTURAL VOCABULARY AND UNDERSTANDING

ADULTERY: As defined by the Jewish law, adultery is the unlawful intercourse of a man with a married or betrothed woman not his own. It was expressly forbidden in the seventh of the Ten Commandments given to Moses. Abraham and Sarah, of course, lived centuries before Moses. Nevertheless, bigamy or polygamy was never God's intention. There are no examples in Scripture that present positive results arising from a sexual relationship between a man and anyone other than his wife. In Abram's case, Hagar was the maidservant of Sarai. As such, Hagar was considered the property of Sarai, and Sarai had full legal authority to do with Hagar as she liked—including giving her to Abram as a vessel through which Abram might bear a son. Although such a son would have Hagar as its biological mother, Sarai had full rights of *authority* over the child because the child was an extension of her property. In similar fashion, Leah and Rachel later gave their maids to Jacob, who was the grandson of Abraham and Sarah. The children born to Bilhah and Zilpah, the maids, were considered full heirs of Jacob, but they were children under the maternal authority of Leah and Rachel.

CONSIDER: Many people in our culture consider adultery benign and normal. What might be done to reestablish an understanding that adultery *always* impacts a family in a negative way?

RESPONDING IN PRAYER

Dear Lord, help me today to focus on what You have given to me and what You have allowed me to accomplish by Your grace. Help me to keep my eyes on what You have promised in Your Word, not upon my prevailing circumstances. In our Lord Jesus' name. Amen.

DAILY ASSIGNMENT

Day Two—A Purpose and a Destiny

The Lord's purpose in choosing and calling Abraham was to make him the father of a great nation that would be His witness to the world. That nation, Israel, would be formally covenanted with Yahweh. Through them, the truth would be kept alive and preserved in perpetuity. From the nation that came out of Abraham, prophets would arise. Through them the Scriptures would be given to the world. God would dwell in their midst and set His sanctuary among them. By their lineage a Deliverer, the Messiah, would arise. And in Him, all the nations of the world would be blessed (Gen. 18:18). Sarah obviously had a key role to play in this plan. Abraham could never become the patriarch of a great nation if she did not first become mother to his offspring.

1. REFLECT: What pressures are on a woman who is married to a man in whom she perceives a great destiny?

   REFLECT: To what degree is a wife called to help her husband fulfill his destiny?

   To what degree must a wife's destiny be embedded within her husband's destiny?

RESPOND: Do you believe that God has given you a great purpose and destiny?

Describe it in a few sentences.

In what ways are you being challenged to fulfill your purpose or destiny?

2. REFLECT: To what extent does having an awareness of a God-given purpose or destiny give a woman both a degree of resiliency and a degree of flexibility?

RESPOND: In what ways are you trusting God to reveal your purpose on earth?

In what ways are you trusting God to help you be *resilient* and *flexible* as you face the future?

RESPONDING IN PRAYER

Jesus, I am trusting You today to help me understand and fully embrace the plan and purpose You have for my life and for my husband's life. Show me the part You desire for me to play in helping my husband fulfill Your call on His life. Show me the ways in which You desire for me to become both more resilient and more flexible as I adapt to the changes that are necessary for us both to fulfill Your destiny for our family. In our Lord Jesus' name. Amen.

DAILY ASSIGNMENT
Day Three—Natural Means and Divine Promises
As she considered her circumstances, Sarah concluded that a kind of surrogate parenting was the only possible solution to her predicament. If God's promise to Abraham were ever going to be fulfilled, Abraham *had* to father children by some means. Sarah thus took it upon herself to try to engineer a fulfillment of the divine promise to Abraham. She unwittingly stepped into the role of God.

1. REFLECT: How difficult is it to continue to trust God to fulfill a promise when every prospect of a *natural* fulfillment of the prophecy seems to be exhausted?

   RESPOND: Have you or someone you know ever been in a situation in which every potential solution seemed to have been tried with no success? What were the emotions related to that realization?

   What might you do to strengthen your faith to withstand years of discouragement or seemingly dead-end efforts?

2. REFLECT: Prior to Hagar's pregnancy, Sarah never had received a promise from God, nor was she specifically named in the covenant God made with Abraham. God never had told Abraham that Sarah would be the matriarch of the nation God promised him. In what ways, and why, is it important for a wife to root her hope and expectation in a promise that she sees as including *her*?

RESPOND: In what ways might the Lord be challenging you to trust Him for a promise related to your life?

RESPONDING IN PRAYER

Heavenly Father, help me to trust You fully in the situations that seem to have no earthly potential for a positive outcome. Help me to look to You rather than my circumstances. In our Lord Jesus' name. Amen.

DAILY ASSIGNMENT

Day Four—An Inability to Hide

Sarah's laughter (just like Abraham's, earlier) seems to have been an exclamation of joy and amazement rather than doubt. Yet when the Lord asked, "Why did Sarah laugh?" she denied it. That denial was motivated by fear. She was afraid because she had not laughed aloud, but within herself. As soon as she realized this stranger had such a sure and thorough knowledge of her heart, she knew instantly and definitively that it was the Lord.

1. REFLECT: Sarah tried to hide when she was confronted with the truth about her behavior. In what ways do we seek to hide or to deny when we are found out?

   What happens when we openly admit to God something He already knows but which we have tried to keep under wraps?

   RESPOND: What is something that you need to openly admit to God?

2. REFLECT: Sarah came face to face with the truth that the Lord sees the heart, not just our behavior. How do you feel knowing that God understands everything about you, including your seemingly hidden motives and secret desires?

Why?

REFLECT: How are the words of a prophet confirmed?

RESPOND: Is there a denial or a fear that you need to confront—especially something you may be attempting to deny to God or a fear that you may have about God?

RESPONDING IN PRAYER
Heavenly Father, I admit to you that sometimes I am afraid of disappointing You or of experiencing Your displeasure. Help me to see you as my loving heavenly Father who always has my best eternal interests at the center of Your plan for me. In our Lord Jesus' name. Amen.

DAILY ASSIGNMENT
Day Five—Protecting the Promise
After seeing Ishmael scoffing at her toddler son, Isaac, she insisted that Abraham cast out the bondwoman. Was Sarah really being overly harsh? In truth, she was not. Ishmael was a threat to God's purpose for Abraham's line as long as he remained in any position to claim that *he*, rather than Isaac, was Abraham's rightful heir. So what may appear at first glance to be an extreme overreaction was actually another proof of Sarah's great faith in God's promise.

1. REFLECT: Sarah actively sought to protect and preserve what had been promised to her and to Abraham by God. In what ways are we entrusted with the responsibility of protecting and preserving those things that God has entrusted to us?

   REFLECT: What is required before a person takes an active step in confronting a threat to a godly person or a godly institution?

   RESPOND: What is something that needs to be cast out of your life before true righteousness can be established? What is the Lord calling you to do?

2. REFLECT: How does God's demand for righteousness run into direct opposition with the world's demand for tolerance of the unrighteous?

   RESPOND: What is an area of your life or an issue in your community that the Lord seems to be calling you to confront in order to protect and preserve what is godly and righteous?

   How might you go about such a confrontation?

RESPONDING IN PRAYER

Dear Lord, please give me Your wisdom so I will know what to protect and preserve with all my heart, soul, and strength . . . and what I might discard freely and quickly so that I might have only *what You desire in my life and home. I ask this in our Lord Jesus' name. Amen.*

3

RAHAB:
A HORRIBLE LIFE REDEEMED

Salmon begot Boaz by Rahab, Boaz begot Obed by Ruth, Obed begot Jesse, and Jesse begot David the king.

(MATT. 1:5–6)

READ

READING ASSIGNMENT
Read Chapter 3 of *Twelve Extraordinary Women*.

BIBLICAL FOCUS
Key passages related to this section of the book: Joshua 2; Joshua 6:22–25; Hebrews 11:31; and James 2:25.

REVIEW

ANOTHER LOOK
The following questions will help you review the material in Chapter 3.

1. How would you describe the spiritual make-over of Rahab to a friend who had never heard the story of Rahab's life (25 words or less)?

2. In what way was Rahab like the Israelites who came to conquer her city?

3. How had Rahab's heart been prepared to believe in Yahweh?

4. What was the motivating force that caused Rahab to hide the Israelite spies?

ADDING TO YOUR SCRIPTURAL VOCABULARY AND UNDERSTANDING

FAITH: Faith is the most solid possible conviction or belief based upon divine assurance, not on empirical evidence. A degree or measure of faith is a gift of God to every person. In other words, every person has some ability to believe, and it is only when that ability is exercised by an act of the will that a person can experience the fruits that arise from having faith. Faith is activated in the human heart by the Holy Spirit through the Word of God and the grace of Jesus Christ.

CONSIDER: Why is it inaccurate for a person to say, "I don't have any faith"?

5. What was the deal that Rahab struck with the Israelite spies?

6. What was the significance of Rahab's hanging a scarlet cord in her window?

7. In what practical ways did Rahab manifest faith?

BIBLE CONNECTIONS

These questions give you an opportunity to reflect on specific biblical passages associated with this lesson.

1. Read Deuteronomy 18:12, 20:17–18 and 1 Kings 21:26. What is your response to the order of God to the Israelites to "utterly destroy" people such as the Amorites, "lest they teach you to do according to all their abominations which they have done for their gods, and you sin against the LORD your God"?

2. Read Numbers 13–15 and Joshua 2:1, 24. Joshua was one of the two spies who returned with a good report after being sent by Moses to do reconnaissance in the Promised Land. In preparing the Israelites to conquer the Promised Land, Joshua sent two spies into Jericho. Compare these two incidents. In what ways are they similar?

How are they different?

What are the implications for today as we "scout out" areas of evil for conquest with the gospel?

3. Read Joshua 2:4–7 and Proverbs 12:22. Rahab told a lie in protecting the Israelite spies. Respond to this statement: "Scripture never commends the lie. Rahab isn't applauded for her ethics. Rahab is a positive example of faith."

How would you reply to a person who said to you, "Rahab's lie is a matter of situational ethics. Sometimes the end justifies the means"?

4. Read Psalm 145:6. To what awesome act in your life might you point as an example of God's greatness?

5. Read Romans 8:28. In what ways is Rahab an example of God's Word that "all things work together for good to those who love God, to those who are called according to His purpose"?

6. Read Mark 2:17. In what ways is Rahab an example of Jesus' words that He "did not come to call the righteous, but sinners, to repentance"?

HIGHLIGHTING THE LESSON

1. Rahab's life is a vivid example that even the worst of sinners can be redeemed by divine grace through faith. Why is it important that we never lose sight of this truth?

2. Rahab was not redeemed by any meritorious works she did. She did not earn God's favor by any good deeds. Remember, even what she *did* do right— harboring the spies—was morally tainted because of the way she handled it. She lied. But she is not given to us as an example of the power of human works. She is not a lesson in self-improvement. She is a reminder that God by His grace can redeem even the most horrible life. Why is it important that we remember always that "by grace you have been saved through faith, and that not of yourselves; it is the gift of God, not of works, lest anyone should boast. For we are *His* workmanship"(Eph, 2:8–10, emphasis added)?

LASTING IMPLICATIONS

1. The Amorite culture in Jericho had reached God's maximum tolerance level. How might we determine the maximum tolerance level God has for any group of people?

What is the best way to avoid even approaching God's maximum tolerance to evil?

2. The Amorite culture in which Rahab lived was devoted to the pursuit of carnal self-gratification and her livelihood as a prostitute was totally dependent on consensual evil. How would you describe the culture in which you live?

Are there professions today, apart from prostitution, that are totally dependent on consensual evil?

We seem to live in a culture that believes if both people are in agreement about a behavior, that behavior isn't a sin. Why is this untrue?

As Christians, what should be our response to consensual evil acts in our society?

3. Rahab had an opportunity to hear about the God of the Israelites long before two spies came to her door. In what ways are we each responsible for communicating the gospel to our nation so that God might use the presentation of His Word to touch the hearts of the unsaved?

REFLECT AND RESPOND

DAILY ASSIGNMENT
Day One—No "Redeeming" Qualities

As far as the record of her life is concerned, there were no redeeming qualities whatsoever about Rahab's life up to this point. On the contrary, she would have been in the very basement of the moral hierarchy in a Gentile culture that was itself as thoroughly degenerate and as grossly pagan as any society in world history. She was a moral bottom-feeder. She made her living off that culture's insatiable appetite for unbridled debauchery, catering to the most debased appetites of the very dregs of society. It is hard to imagine a more unlikely candidate for divine honor than Rahab.

1. REFLECT: Have you ever met or known a woman who seemed to have *no* redeeming qualities?

   How did you feel or how do you believe you would have felt upon hearing that this woman had accepted Jesus Christ as her personal Savior?

   REFLECT: What do you consider to be *your* redeeming qualities?

   Why?

   How did these qualities come into play in your salvation experience?

RESPOND: How is the Lord challenging you to adjust your thinking about who might be saved? How might your new perspective affect your attitude and actions?

2. REFLECT: As an Amorite woman growing up and living in Jericho, could Rahab have lived a life different than the one she had lived prior to hearing about the God of the Israelites?

REFLECT: To what extent are women today who have never heard about Jesus responsible for their moral choices or their responses to God?

RESPOND: What does the story of the life of Rahab say to you about your life?

How might you take action on what you are thinking or feeling?

RESPONDING IN PRAYER
Dear Lord, help me today to see other people as You see them. Help me never to define someone as beyond the reach of Your grace. In our Lord Jesus' name. Amen.

DAILY ASSIGNMENT
Day Two—Confluent Forces for Good
It is an unlikely confluence of forces for good—on the one hand, a lone pagan woman whose life up until now had been anything but heroic, and an entire nation of itinerant, lifelong refugees who had lived for the past forty years under the frown of God

because of their parents' disobedience. But the spies' collaboration with Rahab was the beginning of the downfall of Jericho. Jericho's defeat was the first dramatic conquest in one of history's greatest military campaigns ever.

1. REFLECT: In looking back over your life and your spiritual journey, what were the "confluent forces for good" in your experience?

   RESPOND: How might you *be* a force for good in the life of someone who does not yet know Jesus as Savior?

2. REFLECT: To what extent is the "working of all forces for good" in a person's life the sovereign work of God alone?

   In what ways can we err by trying to engineer the salvation of another person?

   In what ways can we err by saying or doing nothing to share the gospel with a person who has not received Christ?

   RESPOND: What specific person is the Lord bringing to your mind as you reflect on God's grace in weaving together "confluent forces for good"?

What do you believe the Lord wants you to do?

RESPONDING IN PRAYER

Jesus, help me to do what You desire for me to do to be a force for good in other people's lives. Show me how to work within Your plan and as an instrument of Your grace. Help me never to get ahead of You or lag behind Your work on this earth. In our Lord Jesus' name. Amen.

DAILY ASSIGNMENT

Day Three—A Healthy Fear

Aside from Rahab herself, the people of Jericho do not seem to have been sufficiently fearful of Yahweh's power or Israel's military might. Perhaps the tales about forty years of aimless wandering had a tendency to counterbalance the Canaanites' fear over Israel's military might. Whatever the reason for their complacency, residents of Jericho were obviously too smug in the security of their walled fortress.

1. REFLECT: What is the difference between having a healthy fear of God and being so scared of God that you don't want a relationship with Him?

    REFLECT: Have you ever been overly afraid of God? What was the outcome of your fear?

    Have you ever been insufficiently afraid of God? What was the outcome?

RESPOND: How is the Lord challenging you to adjust your beliefs regarding what it means to be "fearful" of the Him? What do you believe you must do?

2. REFLECT: In this day and age, when our society seemingly desires only a God of love and mercy and not a God of justice, many people do not seem to be sufficiently fearful of the consequences associated with disobeying God's commandments or being disrespectful to God. How do you define "sufficiently fearful"?

REFLECT: Who or what instills a sufficient fear of the Lord?

RESPOND: As you reflect upon what it means to have a fear of the Lord, what is something you believe you must change in your life?

RESPONDING IN PRAYER

Heavenly Father, You are awesome and almighty—the sovereign King of the universe with all power and authority. You are just and demand justice. Help me to remember always that You require respect and righteous behavior from those who are in relationship with You. Help me to model a healthy fear of You in all I say and do. In our Lord Jesus' name. Amen.

DAILY ASSIGNMENT

Day Four—Fear that Produces Faith

In Rahab's case, fear is partly what motivated her faith. She had heard powerful evidence of the Lord's supremacy over Egypt. She understood that it was the Lord's might (not sheer military skill) that had triumphed over Sihon and Og, two fearsome Amorite kings. She probably understood something of Yahweh's sovereign authority over Israel from the tales of their forty years in the wilderness. Hers was a healthy kind of fear. It had convinced her that Yahweh was indeed the one true God.

1. REFLECT: Why is it important that we openly recognize that the Lord alone has delivered us from evil and allows us to live to this moment?

   REFLECT: For what reasons is it important that we openly recognize that God is in control of all things and that He alone has sovereign authority over our lives?

   RESPOND: To whom should you speak about God's saving, delivering power over your life?

2. REFLECT: In what ways does healthy fear produce faith?

   RESPOND: Based on the story of Rahab, what might you trust God to do in your life today?

RESPONDING IN PRAYER

Heavenly Father, help me to be ever mindful of all the many ways in which you have delivered me from evil in the past. Help me to trust You today as the One who is in control of all things in my life. In our Lord Jesus' name. Amen.

DAILY ASSIGNMENT

Day Five—Faith Coupled with Works

Rahab's faith did not lie dormant long. Remember, it was only after she hid the spies that she verbalized to them her belief that Yahweh was the one true God. Her faith was seen in the fruit of her works before she even had an opportunity to verbalize it on her tongue. James says genuine faith is always active and fruitful like that. "Faith without works is dead" (James 2:26). Rahab's faith was anything but dead.

1. REFLECT: How was Rahab's faith manifested to the Israelite spies?

   REFLECT: How was Rahab's faith manifested after the spies left?

   RESPOND: In what ways is the Lord challenging you to make your faith more active and fruitful?

2. REFLECT: Rahab found herself living the rest of her days among the Israelites. She married an Israelite and had at least one son. How do you believe Rahab's faith might have been challenged and manifested as a woman suddenly living in a new culture with new religious traditions?

   REFLECT: What challenges did you face as you adapted to a new way of living after you accepted Jesus as your Savior?

RESPOND: How is the Lord using the story of Rahab to inspire you to express your faith in new ways?

RESPONDING IN PRAYER

Dear Lord, I deeply desire to have an active faith that produces life-giving works. Show me how to put hands and feet and voice to my faith. I ask this in our Lord Jesus' name. Amen.

4

RUTH: LOYALTY AND LOVE

Your people shall be my people, and your God, my God.

(RUTH 1:16)

READ

READING ASSIGNMENT
Read Chapter 4 of *Twelve Extraordinary Women*.

BIBLICAL FOCUS
Key passages related to this section of the book: Book of Ruth.

REVIEW

ANOTHER LOOK
The following questions will help you review the material in Chapter 4.

1. Prior to her meeting Boaz, how was Ruth a "fitting picture of every sinner"?

2. As a Moabite woman, how might Ruth initially have been perceived by the Israelite family of Elimelech and Naomi?

3. Describe Naomi's life during the time she decided to return to Israel from Moab.

4. Compare the responses of Orpah and Ruth when Naomi encouraged them to return to their families rather than follow her to Israel.

How do you believe you might have responded to Naomi?

5. In what ways did Boaz show special kindness to Ruth as she gleaned?

In what ways did Ruth gain even greater affection and assistance from Boaz?

In what ways is Boaz like the Lord in His provision for us as we work in His fields?

In what ways should we be like Ruth in our appreciation and thanksgiving to the Lord?

6. The Hebrew word *goel* is translated in the New King James Version of the Bible as "one of our close relatives." The *goel* was a relative who came to the rescue. The word *goel* includes the idea of redemption, or deliverance. Write a brief definition of this word in your own terms, and especially as you understand Jesus Christ to be your *goel.*

7. Briefly summarize the way in which Ruth proposed marriage to Boaz.

BIBLE CONNECTIONS

These questions give you an opportunity to reflect on specific biblical passages associated with this lesson.

1. Read Ruth 1:15. Naomi said of Orpah, that she had "gone back to her people and to her gods." In what way might Naomi have been testing the faith of Ruth in pointing out that Orpah had returned to worship the Moabite gods?

2. Read Ruth 1:20–21. Naomi, whose name means "pleasant," wanted the people of Bethlehem to call her Mara, which means "bitter." In calling herself Mara, she was not suggesting that she had become a bitter person; but (as her words reveal) that Providence had handed her a bitter cup to drink. She saw the hand of God in her sufferings, but far from complaining, she was simply acknowledging her faith in the sovereignty of God, even in the midst of a life of bitter grief. In what ways is it possible to remain a person of faith even as you acknowledge that the circumstances and situations of your life are *not* pleasant?

Give an example from your own life or the life of someone you know.

ADDING TO YOUR SCRIPTURAL VOCABULARY AND UNDERSTANDING

GLEANING: In the time of Ruth, all harvest of grain crops was done strictly by hand. As a result, heads of grain often fell to the ground as the sheaves of wheat, barley, or corn were cut from their roots. According to the Law of Moses, the poor were to be allowed to gather the gleanings of the field, as well as the unharvested remains of vineyards and olive groves. This allowed the poor an opportunity to engage in honest labor and to gather the grain that would feed their families. Those who gleaned from the fields not only picked up the fallen grains from the field, but were responsible for separating their own grain from the chaff at the threshing floors. In many cases the corners of a field were left completely unharvested so that the poor might glean there.

CONSIDER: In what ways was gleaning beneficial to the Israelite society?

3. Read Matthew 1:5. In what ways did Boaz' familiarity with the life story of Rahab make him more prone to extend special care to a foreign woman like Ruth?

In what ways was Ruth's faith reminiscent of Rahab's?

4. Read Leviticus 19:9–10; 23:22; and Deuteronomy 24:19–21. What is the balance in Scripture between requiring work from the poor and providing opportunity to the poor?

HIGHLIGHTING THE LESSON

1. The Book of Ruth is a wonderful story about love between a young woman and her mother-in-law, and between a young woman and a noble man who provided for her. In what ways is it also a love story between God and His people?

2. It took faith, courage, and effort for Ruth to leave Moab and travel to Israel. It took faith, courage, and effort for Ruth to embrace the God of Israel, the people of Israel, and to support her mother-in-law by physically demanding field labor. It took faith, courage, and effort for Ruth to approach Boaz as her *goel* and to trust him to do the right thing by her. In what ways does the Lord require each of us to exhibit faith, courage, and effort as we follow the Lord Jesus Christ?

LASTING IMPLICATIONS

1. The fact that Elimelech would take his family to Moab is a measure of the famine's frightening severity. The land of Israel was evidently both spiritually and physically parched, and times were desperate. Is there ever any justification for the saying, "desperate times call for desperate measures"?

   If a woman finds herself or her family in an ungodly environment because of life-or-death circumstances, how should she respond?

2. God made a way in the life of Ruth and Naomi when there seemed to be no way. In what ways does God ask each of us to trust Him to provide for us all that we need, in precisely the way and in precisely the right time, in order to accomplish *His* purposes in our lives?

REFLECT AND RESPOND

DAILY ASSIGNMENT
Day One—When Things Go from Bad to Worse
Naomi, Elimelech, and their two sons, Mahlon and Chilion, had gone to Moab in a time of famine in the area of Bethlehem. Elimelech died in Moab leaving Naomi a widow.

Then both Mahlon and Chilion died, leaving the three women to fend for themselves. In that culture, this was a nearly impossible situation. Three widows, with no children and no responsible relatives, in a time of famine, could not hope to survive for long, even if they pooled their meager resources. We're not told what caused any of the husbands to die, but the fact that all three perished is a measure of how hard life was in the adversity of those days. Mahlon and Chilion seem to have died in quick succession, suggesting they perhaps fell victim to a disease, very likely related to the famine.

1. REFLECT: What emotions might these women have felt as they dealt with famine and the sudden deaths of their spouses, and in Naomi's case her only sons?

In what ways and over what were they likely to be grieving?

REFLECT: Describe a time when you or someone you know experienced a situation in which a sequence of negative events led to the "brink of ruin"?

RESPOND: Is there someone in a desperate time of trouble that the Lord is bringing to your mind and heart right now? If so, what might you do to reach out to that person?

RESPONDING IN PRAYER
Dear Lord, help me to trust You even when bad things happen to good people. Show me how to reach out to someone who is feeling devastated or in despair today. Help me to show the love of Christ to that person. I ask this in our Lord Jesus' name. Amen.

DAILY ASSIGNMENT
Day Two—The Spiritual Struggle During Hard Times
As she advised her daughters-in-law to return to their families rather than follow her back to Israel, Naomi said to them: "the hand of the Lord has gone out against me." Naomi no doubt struggled with bitter regret over having come to Moab in the first place. She seems to have been overcome with remorse and perhaps a feeling that she had somehow incurred the Lord's displeasure by going to Moab.

1. REFLECT: Have you or someone you know ever perceived negative circumstances as the Lord's punishing you? How does a person determine if he or she is experiencing the consequences of bad choices or sin, or if he or she is simply experiencing the problems that are common to life in a fallen world?

    RESPOND: As you have reflected on the questions above, how has the Lord been speaking to your heart and mind?

2. REFLECT: Words used to describe Naomi are "bitter regret," "remorse," and "anguish." What might a woman do *spiritually* to overcome these deeply wounding emotions?

    RESPOND: Is there a person whom you know today who is struggling with regret, remorse, or deep anguish? If so, what might you do to help?

RESPONDING IN PRAYER

Lord Jesus, show me Your purposes and the lessons You desire for me to learn when I go through hard times. Help me to be a source of encouragement and spiritual help to others who are feeling regret, remorse, or anguish. Help me to be a vessel of healing and emotional strength to those in need. I pray this in Your name, Lord Jesus. Amen.

DAILY ASSIGNMENT

Day Three—A Pledge of Loyalty and Love
Ruth's reply is a beautiful piece of Hebrew poetry:

LOYALTY AND LOVE

Entreat me not to leave you,
Or to turn back from following after you;
For wherever you go, I will go;
And wherever you lodge, I will lodge;
Your people shall be my people,
And your God, my God.
Where you die, I will die.
And there will I be buried.
The LORD do so to me, and more also,
If anything but death parts you and me.
(Ruth 1:16–17)

1. REFLECT: Circle the words or phrases in the passage above that stand out to you. Pause to consider why these particular words or phrases seem to have extra meaning to you.

REFLECT: What are the hallmarks of loyalty expressed in this reply by Ruth?

REFLECT: In what ways is Ruth's response a great proclamation of faith in the God of Israel?

REFLECT: Why was it important for Naomi to know that Ruth was committed to the God of Israel before Ruth returned with her to Bethlehem?

RESPOND: What might keep you from being able to make such a pledge of loyalty to your spouse, friend, or relative? Are there areas of pain in your relationship that you need to address or to forgive? Do you need to make amends with another person? How is the Lord dealing with you right now?

RESPONDING IN PRAYER

Heavenly Father, I want to be a person who openly and genuinely is loyal and loving. Show me areas in my life that I need to address. Help me to make the changes I need to make—to forgive what I need to forgive, to seek forgiveness from those I have hurt, and to allow You to heal any brokenness within me that holds me back from "moving forward in faith" toward all that You have for me. I pray this in our Lord Jesus' name. Amen.

DAILY ASSIGNMENT

Day Four—Willing to Glean

In agreeing to return to Bethlehem with Naomi, Ruth was agreeing to help support the aging woman. The biblical data suggest that Ruth was still quite young and physically strong. So she went to work in the fields, gleaning what the harvesters left behind in order to provide enough grain to eke out an existence.

1. REFLECT: In the previous lesson about Rahab we noted the importance of adding works to your faith. In what ways was Ruth adding works to her love and loyalty?

    REFLECT: How was Ruth's willingness to work in the fields as a common field laborer an expression of faith?

    REFLECT: Ruth's behavior is in sharp contrast to those who want "something from nothing" or those who think they are "too good to work." How do you personally feel about the importance of work and the need to take personal responsibility for supporting yourself and your family?

RESPOND: Is there a field in which the Lord is asking you to work today?

RESPONDING IN PRAYER

Heavenly Father, show me what to do and where to go so that I might fulfill the purpose that You have for me on this earth. Lead me to the harvest fields in which I might gather or glean. Help me never to become too proud to do even the most menial task. In our Lord Jesus' name. Amen.

DAILY ASSIGNMENT

Day Five—Bold but Virtuous Plans

Naomi's scheme was bold and utterly unconventional. Of course, Ruth, as a foreigner, could always plead ignorance of Jewish custom, but if Naomi's plan had been known in advance by people in the community, the propriety police certainly would have been up in arms. Of course, the scheme did not involve any *real* unrighteousness or indecency. Naomi certainly would not have asked Ruth to compromise her virtue or relinquish godly modesty.

1. REFLECT: How important was it that Ruth not act on her own, but rather take the advice of the older and wiser Naomi?

REFLECT: Very often we equate bold and unconventional with being "slightly sinful" or being "too aggressive." Why did this particular situation with Boaz seem to call for bold and unconventional methodology?

RESPOND: Do you have a need that might require a bold but virtuous plan for solving it? If so, what might you do to initiate that plan?

2. REFLECT: Note that Ruth gleaned in Boaz' fields until the "end of barley harvest and wheat harvest" (Ruth 2:23). These harvests were weeks apart. How does the passage of time and the precision of timing factor into the bold but virtuous plan that Naomi developed for Ruth?

RESPOND: How critical is timing to *your* bold but virtuous plan? In what specific ways is the Lord directing you regarding the precise timing for your plan?

RESPONDING IN PRAYER

Dear Lord, You see the need in my life and You know that I have been patient in waiting for the right time to take action. Now I feel that You are directing me to take a bold and courageous step. Please help me to listen closely to Your precise timing and methods. Please give me the courage I need to follow through on this plan You have given me. Please help me always to do all *things in a way that is without sin and that brings honor and glory to You. I ask this in our Lord Jesus' name. Amen.*

5

HANNAH: A PORTRAIT OF FEMININE GRACE

Hannah prayed and said: "My heart rejoices in the Lord; My horn is exalted in the Lord. I smile at my enemies, Because I rejoice in Your salvation.

(1 SAMUEL 2:1)

READ

READING ASSIGNMENT
Read Chapter 5 of *Twelve Extraordinary Women.*

BIBLICAL FOCUS
Key passages related to this section of the book: 1 Samuel 1:1–2:10 and 1 Samuel 2:18–21.

REVIEW

ANOTHER LOOK
The following questions will help you review the material in Chapter 5.

1. In what ways did Hannah fit the meaning of her name, "grace"?

2. In what ways was Hannah like both Sarah and Mary the mother of Jesus?
   • Sarah

   • Mary

3. Based on what Scripture says, describe the outset of Hannah's life.

4. What were the three great loves of Hannah's life?

5. Why did Hannah long to have a son?

6. Describe Hannah's prayer life, specifically her prayer at the entrance to the door of the tabernacle.

7. What traits of God did Hannah include in her great prayer of thanksgiving and praise found in 1 Samuel 2:1–10?

What traits about humanity did Hannah include in her prayer?

What did Hannah pray regarding unbelief and rebellion?

8. Describe Hannah's ongoing relationship with Samuel after she gave him to full-time service at the tabernacle.

9. In what ways was Hannah rewarded for her gift of Samuel to the Lord's service?

BIBLE CONNECTIONS

These questions give you an opportunity to reflect on specific biblical passages associated with this lesson.

1. Read 1 Samuel 1:7 and Numbers 18:24–32. What brought Hannah "year by year" to the house of the LORD?

2. Read 1 Samuel 1:3 and 1 Samuel 2:13–24. In addition to the bad behavior of the high priest's sons, Hophni and Phineas, the visible manifestation of God's glory that once resided over the ark of the covenant was long gone from the tabernacle. What emotions did Hannah and others in her family likely have as they made their annual trip to the tabernacle at Shiloh?

3. Read 1 Samuel 1:4–5. Elkanah gave one portion of offering to Peninnah and all her sons and daughters, and a double portion to Hannah. What emotional difficulties in Elkanah's family might have grown from this discrepancy in "portions" given to his two wives?

What damage is caused by expressions of favoritism in a family?

4. Read 1 Samuel 1:18. Also read Psalm 55:22 and 1 Peter 5:6–7. In what ways was Hannah's reply to the high priest Eli an expression of faith?

5. Read 1 Samuel 2:1–10. List the key words and phrases in Hannah's prayer.

Pause to consider why each of these words has special meaning to you at this time. Make additional comments next to each key word or phrase.

6. Read Proverbs 22:6. What is involved in *training* a child?

HIGHLIGHTING THE LESSON

1. Hannah is a supreme model of devotion to home and motherhood. What are the lessons about the role of a wife and mother that you have gained from a study of her life?

2. What are the main spiritual lessons you have gained from a study of Hannah's life? (Touch upon these areas: devotion, faith, prayer, and dedication.)

LASTING IMPLICATIONS

1. How important are mothers to the ongoing strength of a culture or society?

   How important are mothers to the ongoing strength of the church?

2. What does the life of Hannah say to a society that undervalues the role of mothers or discounts the influence of mothers in the early development of their children?

REFLECT AND RESPOND

DAILY ASSIGNMENT

Day Two—Even in the "Best" of Families

Although Hannah was the wife of a Levite, living in a devout family, and although Hannah knew that her husband loved her deeply, "Hannah's home life was often troubled and sorrowful. Her husband was a bigamist." In the words of Scripture, "He had two wives: the name of one was Hannah, and the name of the other Peninnah. Peninnah had children, but Hannah had no children" (1 Sam. 1:2). Obviously, this situation caused severe tension in the family. Peninnah—called Hannah's "rival" (v. 6)—deliberately provoked her, goading her about the fact that the Lord had withheld children from her.

1. REFLECT: People often believe that Christian families, and especially the families of those in Christian leadership, should be void of problems. That is never the case! All families have problems. Why do you believe even the "best" or "most devout" families sometimes have serious problems?

   REFLECT: What are the consequences associated with the presence of a "second woman" in any marriage?

   RESPOND: Is there a person you know who constantly has to deal with "another woman" in her marriage or home life? If so, what do you believe the Lord desires for you to do to be an encouragement to that woman?

   If you are the person who has to deal with "another woman" in your marriage or home life, what do you believe the Lord is challenging you to do to make this situation better?

2. REFLECT: The Scriptures tells us that Peninnah "provoked [Hannah] severely, to make her miserable" (1 Sam. 1:6). How difficult is it to live or to work with someone who deliberately goads, taunts, or speaks to you derisively with the expressed intent of making you miserable?

REFLECT: How might you have responded to Peninnah in Hannah's place?

ADDING TO YOUR SCRIPTURAL VOCABULARY AND UNDERSTANDING

DOOR OF THE TABERNACLE: The Tabernacle was a tent-like structure made according to the commandments of God given to Moses as the Children of Israel wandered in the wilderness between Egypt and the Promised Land. The Tabernacle was located at the center of the camp of the Israelites and was constructed so that it could be moved readily. The tent itself was surrounded by a courtyard made of fabric and poles. After the Israelites had conquered the Promised Land, the Tabernacle was taken to Shiloh, a centrally located town in Israel, and the courtyard around the tent was apparently made more permanent with fixed walls and pillars. The Tabernacle signified to the Israelites the "location" of God's presence on the earth, even after the ark of the covenant that was historically housed within the Tabernacle—and thought to be the throne of God on the earth—had been captured by the Philistines. Service to the Lord within the Tabernacle courtyard was strictly limited to the Levitical priests. The high priest Eli encountered Hannah "by the door-post of the tabernacle of the LORD" (1 Sam. 1:9). That was as close as Hannah could position herself to what was believed to be the literal presence of God. She was there in an attempt to get as close to Yahweh as possible as she prayed and wept in anguish before the Lord.

CONSIDER: Where do you go to feel close to God?

REFLECT: Why is it that certain people always seem to know how to push our emotional buttons?

In what ways might a person avoid such emotional angst?

RESPOND: As you have studied the life of Hannah, has the Lord brought someone to your mind? If so, what do you believe the Lord is challenging you to?

RESPONDING IN PRAYER

Dear Lord, I confess to You today that there are some people in my life that I simply wish were not there. Even so, I recognize that You have allowed that person to be in my life for a purpose. Help me to see Your plan or lesson in this relationship. Show me how I am to respond with godly virtue, Christian love, and the truth of Your Word. In our Lord Jesus' name. Amen.

DAILY ASSIGNMENT

Day Two—When a Husband's Love Isn't Enough

The Scriptures plainly tell us that Elkanah loved his wife Hannah and that when the time came to make offerings, he gave a double portion to Hannah. Even so, Hannah was in constant anguish because of her own infertility. She longed to be a mother. This was her one ambition in life.

1. REFLECT: Why do you believe Elkanah's deep love wasn't enough to satisfy Hannah?

REFLECT: What are the emotions that a woman has when she deeply desires to be a mother and can't conceive a child or carry a child full-term?

REFLECT: How does a woman feel when the one thing she wants more than anything else is denied to her?

RESPOND: As you have reflected on the questions above, how has the Lord spoken to your heart and mind?

2. REFLECT: Recognizing that not all women are called to be married or to become mothers, how do you respond to this statement: "A woman is by no means required to be a wife or a mother before she can be useful in the Lord's service"?

RESPOND: As you have reflected on the questions above, has the Lord brought a single woman, a childless wife, or a widow to your mind? If so, what might the Lord be asking you to say to that woman?

RESPONDING IN PRAYER

Jesus, help me to base all of my ambitions of life on Your Word and on Your unique and specific plan for my life. Help me to believe for all that You desire for me, and to be satisfied with all that You provide for me. I ask this in Your name, Lord Jesus. Amen.

DAILY ASSIGNMENT

Day Three—A Noble Role

It has been God's plan from the beginning that women should train and nurture godly children and thus leave a powerful imprint on society through the home (1 Tim. 5:10; Titus 2:3–5). Hannah is a classic illustration of how that works. She is a reminder that mothers are the makers of men and the architects of the next generation. Her earnest prayer for a child was the beginning of a series of events that helped turn back the spiritual darkness and backsliding in Israel. She set in motion a chain of events that would ultimately usher in a profound spiritual awakening at the dawn of the Davidic dynasty. We first encounter Hannah when Israel was in desperate need of a great leader and a great man. Hannah became the woman whom God used to help shape that man.

1. REFLECT: What value do you place upon motherhood?

Do you see it as "the highest calling any woman could ever be summoned to"?

REFLECT: In what ways has your perspective of motherhood been impacted by the example of your own mother?

By Scripture?

By societal and cultural pressures?

REFLECT: How do you respond to the statement that motherhood is "the one vocation that God uniquely designed women to fulfill, and no man can ever intrude into the mother's role"?

RESPOND: As you have reflected on the role of motherhood, in what specific ways has the Lord been challenging you?

2. REFLECT: Many mothers have very high expectations for their children. In what ways are the expectations of a mother helpful to the child?

Detrimental to the child?

RESPOND: As you have reflected on the expectations that mothers have for their children, in what specific ways has the Lord been challenging you?

RESPONDING IN PRAYER

Heavenly Father, I deeply desire to be the mother that You desire for me to be—either a mother to natural-born children, fostered or adopted children, or in a spiritual way as a mother to spiritual children. Show me how to be a mother who fulfills the role that You have designed for mothers. Help me always to value the fact that You have made me with a mother's heart. In our Lord Jesus' name. Amen.

DAILY ASSIGNMENT

Day Four—Love and Worship

Hannah's love for her husband is the first key to understanding her profound influence as a mother. Contrary to popular opinion, the most important characteristic of a godly mother is not her relationship with her children. It is her love for her husband. The love between husband and wife is the real key to a thriving family. A healthy home environment cannot be built exclusively on the parents' love for their children. The properly situated family has marriage at the center; families shouldn't revolve around the children. All parents need to heed this lesson: what you communicate to your children through your marital relationship will stay with them for the rest of their lives.

1. REFLECT: The love between Hannah and Elkanah included a shared love for the Lord. They went up yearly to worship and sacrifice to the Lord at Shiloh, and no doubt they made other trips to Shiloh to celebrate the three annual feasts all Israelite men were required to attend. To what extent is worshiping together a natural outgrowth of a deep love between a husband and wife?

   In what ways does worshiping together enhance the love between a husband and wife?

   REFLECT: In what ways are children in a family influenced when they see their parents worshiping God together?

   RESPOND: As you have reflected about the links between family love and worship, what has the Lord been challenging you to do?

2. REFLECT: Hannah deeply desired to have a son because she loved God and desired to give a child to the Lord. How is this motivation toward motherhood different than the motivations of self-gratification or self-fulfillment?

REFLECT: What difference is made in a child's life when that child's mother has deep devotion to the Lord?

REFLECT: What does it mean to dedicate or consecrate a child to the Lord?

How is this dedication or consecration an act of worship?

RESPOND: As you have reflected about the links between worship and a mother's relationship to her children, how has the Lord been challenging you personally?

3 REFLECT: Hannah's immediate response to the dedication of her son Samuel to service in the tabernacle was prayer and praise. In what ways might a mother pray for each of her children every day?

REFLECT: How might a mother's praise to God impact her child's spiritual development?

RESPOND: In what ways is the Lord challenging you to praise Him and to pray for the children in your life?

RESPONDING IN PRAYER
Heavenly Father, show me how I might worship You through the way I relate to my children. Teach me what it means to dedicate my child to Your service with my whole heart. In our Lord Jesus' name. Amen.

DAILY ASSIGNMENT
Day Five—A Mother's Influence

After the birth of her son Samuel, Hannah became the very model of a stay-at-home mom. No mother was ever more devoted to home and child. She had important work to do—nurturing him, caring for him, and helping him learn the most basic truths of life and wisdom. She taught him his first lessons about Yahweh. She made her home an environment where he could learn and grow in safety. And she carefully directed the course of his learning and helped shape his interests.

1. REFLECT: Define the "model mother."

REFLECT: In what ways is it difficult for a mother to entrust her child to the care and teaching of other adults—for example, teachers and Sunday school teachers, other caregivers (such as nannies, babysitters, or day-care workers), and grandparents?

REFLECT: In dealing with her own child, what can a mother teach better than any other person?

RESPOND: As you have reflected on the role of motherhood, how has the Lord been challenging you?

2. REFLECT: When her son was only a toddler, Hannah entrusted him to Eli and to service in the tabernacle. What emotions must Hannah have felt in giving up her son to serve the Lord?

REFLECT: In what ways can a person "give" another person to the Lord?

REFLECT: In what ways do we each struggle when we give to the Lord something of tremendous value?

RESPOND: As you have reflected upon Hannah's gift of her son to the Lord, how has the Lord been challenging you in your giving?

RESPONDING IN PRAYER

Dear Lord, make me a cheerful and willing giver, knowing that all I have is ultimately from You and belongs to You. Help me to be a generous and wise giver to my children— giving to them only what You would give, which is always what is eternally best for them. I ask this in our Lord Jesus' name. Amen.

6

MARY: BLESSED AMONG WOMEN

The virgin's name was Mary. And having come in, the angel said to her, "Rejoice, highly favored one, the Lord is with you: blessed are you among women!"

(LUKE 1:27–28)

READ

READING ASSIGNMENT
Read Chapter 6 of *Twelve Extraordinary Women*.

BIBLICAL FOCUS
Key passages related to this section of the book: Luke 1:26–2:52; John 2:1–5; and John 19:26–27.

REVIEW

ANOTHER LOOK
The following questions will help you review the material in Chapter 6.

1. Of all the women in Scripture, Mary stands out above all others as being the most "blessed." What does the word "blessed" mean to you?

2. What are some of the dangers that arise if Mary is elevated too much?

3. Describe Mary's early years in Nazareth.

4. What was Mary's response to the messages given to her by the angel Gabriel?

5. In what ways was Mary's visit to Elizabeth important for her?

6. What does Mary's praise song, known in Latin as the *Magnificat*, reveal to us about Mary's faith?

7. What attributes of God's nature did Mary include in her song of praise?

8. Mary appeared in only three scenes during Christ's earthly ministry. Briefly identify and describe these incidents.

BIBLE CONNECTIONS

These questions give you an opportunity to reflect on specific biblical passages associated with this lesson.

1. Read Psalm 72:17; Genesis 22:18; and Revelation 19:10. Why is it important to remember always that Jesus, and Jesus alone, is the fountain of grace and the long-awaited Seed of Abraham who is the covenant maker?

2. Read Luke 11:27–28. When admirers of Jesus showed undue reverence to Mary, how did Jesus respond?

ADDING TO YOUR SCRIPTURAL VOCABULARY AND UNDERSTANDING

MAGNIFICAT: This is the name often given to Mary's outpouring of praise to the Lord. The word is Latin in origin. It refers to the opening line of Mary's praise song: "My soul magnifies the Lord" (Luke 1:46).

CONSIDER: How might we do more to "magnify" the Lord in our praise and in our witness?

3. Read Luke 1:28–35. Highlight or mark any words or phrases that stand out to you as you read again the annunciation of the angel Gabriel to Mary. Why do you think these particular words or phrases have special meaning to you?

And having come in, the angel said to her, "Rejoice, highly favored one, the Lord is with you; blessed are you among women!"

But when she saw him, she was troubled at his saying, and considered what manner of greeting this was.

Then the angel said to her, "Do not be afraid, Mary, for you have found favor with God. And behold, you will conceive in your womb and bring forth a Son, and shall call His name Jesus. He will be great, and will be called the Son of the Highest; and the Lord God will give Him the throne of His father David. And He will reign over the house of Jacob forever, and of His kingdom there will be no end."

Then Mary said to the angel, "How can this be, since I do not know a man"?

And the angel answered and said to her, "The Holy Spirit will come upon you, and the power of the Highest will overshadow you; therefore, also, that Holy One who is to be born will be called the Son of God." (Luke 1:28–35)

4. Read Luke 1:46–55. As you read through Mary's song of praise to God, highlight or mark those words or phrases that stand out to you. Why do you think these particular words or phrases have added meaning?

In what specific ways do you believe a person can "magnify" the Lord?

> *My soul magnifies the Lord,*
> *And my spirit has rejoiced in God my Savior.*
> *For He has regarded the lowly state of His maidservant;*
> *For behold, henceforth all generations will call me blessed.*
> *For He who is mighty has done great things for me,*
> *And holy is His name.*
> *And His mercy is on those who fear Him*

From generation to generation.
He has shown strength with His arm;
He has scattered the proud in the imagination of their hearts.
He has put down the mighty from their thrones,
And exalted the lowly.
He has filled the hungry with good things,
And the rich He has sent away empty.
He has helped His servant Israel,
In remembrance of His mercy,
As He spoke to our fathers,
To Abraham and to his seed forever.

(Luke 1:46–55)

5. Read John 2:1–5. Was Jesus being too hard on his mother?

   What do you believe His purpose was in speaking to her as He did?

6. Read Mark 2:31–35. Was Jesus being too dismissive of his family?

   What was His purpose in speaking to Mary and other family members as He did?

What was the message sent to the disciples who heard Him speak to His family?

7. Read Luke 2:19, 51. What does it mean to "ponder" something in your heart?

What types of things can and should a mother "ponder" about her children?

What things are better left unvoiced?

ADDING TO YOUR SCRIPTURAL VOCABULARY AND UNDERSTANDING

KIDDUSHIN: This is the Hebrew word for a legal engagement we call a "betrothal" in English. *Kiddushin* was as legally binding as marriage and usually lasted a full year prior to a wedding. The couple was deemed husband and wife and only a legal divorce could dissolve the marriage contract. During this time the couple lived separately from one another and had no physical relations whatsoever. One of the main reasons for *kiddushin* was to demonstrate the fidelity and commitment of both partners to the marriage prior to the wedding.

CONSIDER: How might we better help those who are preparing for marriage to demonstrate their fidelity and commitment prior to a wedding ceremony?

8. Read Acts 1:14. How do you respond to the fact that Mary was among the disciples who were praying together in Jerusalem at Pentecost?

HIGHLIGHTING THE LESSON

1. Although Mary was the earthly mother of Jesus, she was also His follower and disciple. He was her eternal Lord. She understood and embraced that relationship. She bowed to His authority in heavenly matters just as in His childhood and youth He had been subject to her parental authority in earthly matters (Luke 2:51). As a mother, she had once provided all His needs, but in the ultimate and eternal sense, He was her Savior and provider. In what ways did Mary have a unique relationship with Jesus?

   In what ways is her faith relationship with Him similar to the faith relationship we have with Jesus?

2. Mary knew extreme moments of joy and sorrow, of exhilaration and devastation. What do you believe gave Mary steadiness and steadfastness in her life?

LASTING IMPLICATIONS

1. What is the tension between thinking of Mary as just an ordinary woman and venerating her as an object of worship?

What are the factors that make Mary a woman worthy of emulation, but not worship?

2. Mary had a one-of-kind role to play in history. No other woman before her or since will do what she did. In what ways are we to trust the Lord for His one-of-a-kind plan and purpose for our lives?

REFLECT AND RESPOND

DAILY ASSIGNMENT

Day One—A Humble and Unassuming Young Woman

Far from portraying Mary with a halo and a seraphic stare on her face, Scripture reveals her as an average young girl of common means from a peasants' town in a poor region of Israel, betrothed to a working-class fiancé who earned his living as a carpenter. If you had met Mary before her firstborn Son was miraculously conceived, you might not have noticed her at all. She could hardly have been more plain and unassuming. From everything we know of her background and social standing, not much about her life or her experience so far would be deemed very extraordinary.

1. REFLECT: Why do we have a tendency to elevate certain people into "revered" status when, in reality, they are ordinary human beings who may have been gifted by God in unusual or extraordinary ways?

RESPOND: Is there someone today to whom you are paying undue homage or giving undue reverence? How is the Lord challenging you as you read about Mary?

2. REFLECT: Mary's family tree included well-known Bible heroes. In what ways do illustrious ancestors place additional pressure upon a person?

In what ways might such an ancestry inspire a person?

In what ways does such ancestry bring undue attention or praise from other people?

REFLECT: How do you feel about your own family heritage?

In what way has it been a help or hindrance to you?

REFLECT: In what ways are being sincere, earnestly worshipful, and having a childlike trust of the Lord more important than family ancestry or fame?

REFLECT: How do you believe you would respond if you were unexpectedly thrust into a prominent or prestigious position?

RESPOND: In what ways is the Lord challenging you to accept your unique position before Him, totally on the basis of your own faith and trust and not on the basis of family background or accomplishments?

RESPONDING IN PRAYER

Dear Heavenly Father, help me to fully accept the truth that I am made acceptable in Your sight solely by my faith in the Lord Jesus Christ, and not according to anything related to my family, ancestors, or personal accomplishments. Help me to accept Jesus fully as my Savior and to follow You closely as my Lord. I ask this in our Lord Jesus' name. Amen.

DAILY ASSIGNMENT

Day Two—Encounter with an Angel

We have seen throughout this book how numerous godly women fostered the hope of being the one through whom the Redeemer would come. But the privilege came at a high cost to Mary personally because it carried the stigma of an unwed pregnancy. Although she had remained totally and completely chaste, the world was bound to think otherwise. Even Joseph assumed the worst. Common sense suggests that Mary must have anticipated all these difficulties the moment the angel told her she would conceive a child.

1. REFLECT: How do you believe you would have responded initially to the appearance of an angel telling you that you were "blessed" among women and that you had "found favor with God"?

    Would these initial feelings have been altered any when the angel went on to say, "You will conceive in your womb and bring forth a Son, and shall call His name Jesus"?

REFLECT: If you found yourself in Mary's shoes, how would you have felt when the thought first came to you, "What about Joseph?"

REFLECT: In what ways do you find it difficult to follow what the Lord asks or requires of you without consideration for the opinions of other people?

How difficult is it to lay aside all thought of public reputation or desires to be socially acceptable as you follow Jesus Christ as your Savior?

RESPOND: As you have reflected on Mary's initial response to the angel Gabriel, in what ways has the Lord been challenging you?

2. REFLECT: Mary questioned Gabriel as to "how" but did not question Gabriel about his authenticity as a messenger, the overall "what" (content) of his message, or the awesome challenge of God's plan for her life. In what ways do questions about the specifics of God's plan and purpose often keep a person from embracing the plan fully or trusting the Lord unconditionally?

RESPOND: As you have reflected on the question above, how is the Lord asking you to respond to Him?

RESPONDING IN PRAYER

Dear Lord, help me to lay aside all of my questions and doubts when You call me to undertake a task or mission. Help me to trust You to help me in every way to accomplish what it is that You call me to do. In our Lord Jesus' name. Amen.

DAILY ASSIGNMENT

Day Three—Worshiping with Someone Who Understands

The angel had explicitly informed Mary about Elizabeth's pregnancy. So it was natural for her to seek out a close relative who was both a strong believer and also expecting her first son by a miraculous birth, announced by an angel (Luke 1:13–19). While Elizabeth was much older and had always been unable to conceive, and Mary was at the beginning of life, both had been supernaturally blessed by God to conceive. It was a perfect situation for the two women to spend time rejoicing together in the Lord's goodness to both of them.

1. REFLECT: In what ways is it important for a woman to be able to share her faith experiences with another woman?

   REFLECT: How important is it to have friends who understand what you are going through based upon their personal experiences?

   RESPOND: As you have read and studied the relationship between Elizabeth and Mary, has the Lord brought someone to your mind or heart? Is there someone you believe the Lord desires for you to encourage in her faith walk? In her pregnancy?

   Is there someone to whom you are to go for godly counsel and friendship?

2. REFLECT: In what ways is it valuable to the growth of your own faith to give voice to what you believe about God and His plan and purpose for you?

RESPOND: Create your own expression of praise to the Lord, including what you believe to be God's nature as He has revealed Himself to you, and what you believe to be God's call on your life.

3. REFLECT: In what ways do you feel free, or inhibited, in voicing your praise to God in the presence of other people?

RESPOND: In what ways do you believe the Lord might be challenging you to overcome your personal inhibitions about voicing praise to Him?

RESPONDING IN PRAYER

Jesus, I want to praise You more fully, more completely, and with greater joy. Teach me how to praise You as You desire to be praised. Lead me to a friend with whom I might share my faith and in whose presence I feel free to praise You openly. In our Lord Jesus' name. Amen.

DAILY ASSIGNMENT

Day Four—Establishing Your Praise on Scripture

It is clear that Mary's young heart and mind were already thoroughly saturated with the Word of God. She included not only echoes of two of Hannah's prayers (1 Sam. 1:11, 2:1–10), but also several other allusions to the law, the psalms, and the prophets.

Take a few minutes to review the chart on pages 118–119 in *Twelve Extraordinary Women* that compare Mary's words of praise to Old Testament verses that are similar in content and tone.

1. REFLECT: Mary's song of praise is all about God's greatness. In what ways is it important that our praise to the Lord be "all about Him" and not about us?

   REFLECT: Mary praised the Lord for His faithfulness across the generations. In what ways has the Lord shown His faithfulness in your life and heritage?

   REFLECT: Mary praised the Lord for the "strength of His arm." How has the Lord shown Himself to be all-powerful in your life?

   REFLECT: Mary's praise song was steeped in Scripture. What are some of your favorite verses of Scripture about the goodness and greatness of God?

   RESPOND: Write out several statements of praise to the Lord that flow directly from the Scriptures.

RESPONDING IN PRAYER
Heavenly Father, I praise You today! You alone are worthy of my praise! Let all of my petitions in prayer be rooted in my understanding of Your greatness, goodness, and glory! In our Lord Jesus' name. Amen.

DAILY ASSIGNMENT
Day Five—A Mother All of Jesus' Life
Mary became one of His faithful disciples. She seems to have come to grips with the

reality that He had work to do, and she could not direct it. She ultimately followed Him all the way to the cross.

1. REFLECT: In what ways might it have been difficult for Mary to accept the truth that she had no more claim on Him than anyone else?

    REFLECT: In what ways is it difficult for a mother to accept the reality that her grown child might refuse to be interrupted or sidetracked by her sincere maternal concern?

    REFLECT: In what ways is it difficult for a mother to accept the truth that her children need to be about their heavenly Father's business, and that she needs to trust God's call on her children's lives?

    RESPOND: As you have read and studied about Mary's ongoing relationship with Jesus during His adult years of ministry, in what ways has the Lord been challenging you?

2. REFLECT: In what ways do you believe Mary might have been influenced by what other people said about her Son? Refer specifically to Simeon and Anna (Luke 2:25–38).

REFLECT: In what ways do you believe Mary had to adjust her relationship with her Son after He said to her, "Did you not know I must be about My Father's business" (Luke 2:49)?

REFLECT: In what ways have you been influenced to think differently about a child by what other people have said or by what your child may have said to you?

RESPOND: As you have reflected on statements made to Mary, how has the Lord been speaking to your heart and mind?

RESPONDING IN PRAYER

Dear Lord, show me how to be the best mother I can be to my child at every age in his or her life. Reveal to me a glimpse of how You see my child. Show me how to yield control over my adult child's life to You. I ask this in our Lord Jesus' name. Amen.

7

ANNA: THE FAITHFUL WITNESS

She gave thanks to the Lord, and spoke of Him to all those who looked for redemption in Jerusalem.

(LUKE 2:38)

READ

READING ASSIGNMENT
Read Chapter 7 of *Twelve Extraordinary Women.*

BIBLICAL FOCUS
Key passages related to this section of the book: Luke 2:36–38.

REVIEW

ANOTHER LOOK
The following questions will help you review the material in Chapter 7.

1. Who other than Anna recognized Christ at His birth?

On what basis did each person or group recognize Him?

2. Three verses in the Gospel of Luke tell Anna's story. From those verses, what do we know about her?

3. Anna's name means "grace"—in Hebrew her name is identical to "Hannah." In what ways is Anna like Hannah of the Old Testament (studied previously)?

4. How was Anna like or unlike the five women called "prophetesses" in the Old Testament (Miriam, Deborah, Huldah, Noadiah, and Isaiah's wife)?

5. In what ways was Anna uniquely qualified to recognize baby Jesus as the Christ?

6. How does Anna's story reflect a "miracle of timing"?

BIBLE CONNECTIONS

These questions give you an opportunity to reflect on specific biblical passages associated with this lesson.

1. Read Daniel 9:24–27. How do the events of Jesus' birth compare to Daniel's prophecy?

2. Read Luke 3:15 and John 1:27–37. In what ways might a person draw a parallel between those who were anticipating Messiah in the first century and those who are anticipating the Second Coming of Christ?

3. Read Luke 2:25–35; Deuteronomy 19:15; and 2 Corinthians 13:1. How are the words of Simeon and Anna in line with the Law's requirements for the establishment of truth?

   How are the words and deeds of Simeon and Anna similar?

   Different?

HIGHLIGHTING THE LESSON

1. Anna was blessed by God to be one of a handful of key witnesses who knew and understood the significance of Jesus' birth. In what ways are we to know and understand the significance of Jesus Christ in our world today?

2. Anna knew the Word of God, believed it, taught it to other women, and encouraged the faithful worshipers of the temple. How is her life a role model for women who seek to be active in the church today?

LASTING IMPLICATIONS

1. Anna made no attempt to keep what she knew about Jesus a secret. Thus she became one of the first and most enduring witnesses to Christ. What is the challenge we face in becoming enduring witnesses to Christ?

2. Anna's spiritual sensitivity was undoubtedly linked to decades of faithful service in the temple, including prolonged and periodic times of fasting and praying. What lesson does her life give to women today who desire to become spiritually mature and more spiritually sensitive?

REFLECT AND RESPOND

DAILY ASSIGNMENT

Day One—Expecting the Lord to Show Up

It is truly remarkable that when Jesus was born, so few people in Israel recognized their Messiah. It was not as if no one was watching for Him. Messianic expectation in the early first century was running at an all-time high.

Anna's hopes and dreams were full of messianic expectation. She knew the Old Testament promises, and she understood that salvation from sin and the future blessing of Israel depended on the coming of the Messiah. Her longing to see Him was suddenly and surprisingly fulfilled one day as she went about her normal routine in the temple.

1. REFLECT: Historically, the Jewish community had a political and military definition for its Messiah. The Jews were looking for a high-profile person who would arrive with fanfare and pageantry as a conquering king. Given what you know about the birth, life, death, and resurrection of Jesus, how did Jesus fail to meet Jewish messianic expectations?

REFLECT: Do we sometimes expect Jesus to appear in our lives in a particular form or for a particular reason?

REFLECT: How can our preconceived notions sometimes prevent us from seeing the real work that God is doing?

ADDING TO YOUR SCRIPTURAL VOCABULARY AND UNDERSTANDING

PROPHECY: The meaning is simply that of "speaking forth," or "proclaiming publicly," what has already been revealed in the written Word of God. Prophecy is intended to produce a "building up" of a person in the truth, encouragement to obedience, and comfort in times of trouble. As a spiritual gift, prophecy is always for the benefit of the hearer, not the speaker.

CONSIDER: To what extent are we challenged to know the Word of God so that we might "speak it forth" accurately, boldly, and with God's intended purposes?

REFLECT: How do our biases and prejudices sometimes prevent us from seeing people as God sees them?

RESPOND: What preconceived notions, biases, or prejudices keep you from seeing experiences and people as God sees them?

As you have reflected upon and confronted some of your own preconceived perceptions, in what ways is the Lord challenging you?

2. REFLECT: In what ways do we sometimes expect Jesus to appear in our lives only at specially designated times or places?

RESPOND: Anna's longing for the Messiah was fulfilled one day as she went about her normal routine in the temple. Recall a specific incident in which the Lord revealed to you a truth about His character or work as you were going about your normal routine.

In what ways is the Lord challenging you to look for Him among the ordinary situations and experiences of your life?

RESPONDING IN PRAYER

Dear Lord, help me to be on the look out for You in my life today. Help me to lay aside my preconceived notions about what You desire to accomplish in my world, or my preconceived ideas about the ways in which You might work. Open my eyes. I want to see You. I ask this in Your name, Lord Jesus. Amen.

DAILY ASSIGNMENT

Day Two—A Prophetess

What did Luke mean by *prophetess*? He was not suggesting that Anna predicted the future. She was not a fortune-teller. He didn't necessarily even suggest that she received special revelation from God. The word *prophetess* simply designated a woman who spoke the Word of God. Any preacher who faithfully proclaims the Word of God would be a prophet in the general biblical sense. And a prophetess would be a woman uniquely devoted to declaring the Word of God.

Anna may have been a teacher of the Old Testament to other women. Or she may have simply had a private ministry there in the temple offering words of encouragement and instruction from the Hebrew Scriptures to other women who came to worship.

1. REFLECT: In what ways are women uniquely qualified to teach other women?

    REFLECT: For what reasons should every Christian woman read, study, and know the Word of God?

    REFLECT: In what ways are women uniquely qualified to encourage other women in their faith?

RESPOND: As you have reflected on Anna's role as a prophetess, in what ways has the Lord been challenging you?

2. REFLECT: In what ways does God use women as gifted teachers of other women and encouragers of faithful worshipers today?

REFLECT: In what ways does God always have a one-of-a-kind role for each woman He calls to proclaim His Word?

RESPOND: In what ways is the Lord challenging you to explore your unique spiritual gifts?

RESPONDING IN PRAYER
Jesus, show me how You desire to use me to proclaim Your Word today. If there are women I need to teach, lead me to them and guide me in my teaching. If there are faithful worshipers I need to encourage, lead me to them and speak through me to touch their hearts. I ask this in Your name, Lord Jesus. Amen.

DAILY ASSIGNMENT
Day Three—A Woman of Asher
Anna's descent from the tribe of Asher suggests that her heritage owed much to God's grace. She was part of the believing remnant from the northern kingdom, and she was therefore a living emblem of God's faithfulness to His people.

1. REFLECT: Do you or someone you know come from a family that is of another religion, or decidedly non-Christian?

If so, what insights do you have into what it means to be part of a "believing remnant"?

REFLECT: In what ways is it difficult to love and serve the Lord when others around you—in your family, neighborhood, workplace, or culture as a whole—do not know, love, or serve Him?

RESPOND: Is the Lord challenging you to reach out to someone who lives or works in a mostly non-Christian environment? What might you do to encourage or befriend that person?

RESPONDING IN PRAYER

Heavenly Father, please make me increasingly sensitive to people in my sphere of influence—in my neighborhood, extended family, church, workplace, or community—who face a daily challenge of loving and serving You when others around them are opposed to You willfully or unknowingly. Show me how I might encourage those who live and work in non-Christian environments. Strengthen me to be a faithful witness for You regardless of the faith—or lack of faith—in others around me. In our Lord Jesus' name. Amen.

DAILY ASSIGNMENT

Day Four—A Widow Devoted to Prayer and Fasting

By the time of Jesus' birth, Anna was already advanced in years. She had not enjoyed a particularly easy life. Her whole world was shattered by tragedy when she was still quite young, apparently before she had even borne children. Her husband died seven years after their marriage, and she had remained single ever since. She must have led a very frugal, chaste, and sober life. Anna appears to have lived in modest chambers in the outer courts of the temple.

1. REFLECT: What conclusions might you draw about a woman who has spent more than six decades in prayer and fasting, devoting her entire life to the service and worship of God?

    REFLECT: In what ways might Anna have been uniquely qualified to recognize Jesus?

    REFLECT: In what ways does a habit of prayer and fasting make a person more spiritually sensitive and insightful?

    RESPOND: As you have reflected upon prayer and fasting, in what ways has the Lord been speaking to your heart?

2. REFLECT: Anna no doubt had a remarkable knowledge of spiritual truth as a part of the "believing remnant" (as opposed to the apostate majority), as well as spiritual experience drawn from decades of living in the temple and seeing both priests and worshipers come and go. In what ways was she different from many others around her—especially the scribes, Sadducees, and Pharisees?

RESPOND: In what ways is the Lord challenging you today to remain firmly grounded as a believer who knows God's Word thoroughly?

RESPONDING IN PRAYER

Heavenly Father, show me Your desires for my life. Do You desire that I spend more time in fasting and prayer? Do You desire for me to study Your Word with greater diligence? Show me how You desire to prepare me for the work that You are calling me to do for You. In our Lord Jesus' name. Amen.

DAILY ASSIGNMENT

Day Five—Both an Instant and Ongoing Response

Suddenly everything Anna had been praying and fasting for was right there in front of her face, wrapped in a little bundle in Simeon's arms. By faith, she knew instantly that Simeon's prophecy was true and that God had answered her prayers. She immediately began giving thanks to God, and all those many, many years of petition turned to praise.

Anna continually spoke of Him to all who were looking for the Redeemer. This became her one message for the rest of her life. Notice that Anna knew who the believing remnant were. She could identify the *true* worshipers—the ones who, like her, were expectantly awaiting the Messiah. She sought such people out, and at every opportunity from then on, she spoke to them about *Him.*

1. REFLECT: Consider a situation about which you may have been praying for a long time. How will you know that God has answered your prayers?

   REFLECT: Have you or someone you know ever experienced an "instant knowing" that something was true or that a prayer had been answered in a supernatural way? If so, what were the emotions associated with that experience?

How did you or the person you know respond to the moment?

RESPOND: In what ways is the Lord challenging you to be on constant look-out for displays of His awesome handiwork?

2. REFLECT: In what ways does the Lord make the mature believer more sensitive to those who have a spiritual hunger for more of God, or who are ready to receive Jesus as their Savior?

REFLECT: In what ways might a woman become more intentionally sensitive to others who are spiritually seeking or hungry for more of God?

RESPOND: As you have reflected upon our need to be aware continually of ways in which God might use us as mature believers, in what ways has the Lord been speaking to your heart?

RESPONDING IN PRAYER

Dear Lord, I want to recognize You at work in my life and in the lives of others. I want to never stop talking about You. I want to be a faithful witness of Your love and saving grace for the rest of my life. Help me, Lord, to have eyes to see and the courage to speak. I ask this in our Lord Jesus' name. Amen.

8

THE SAMARITAN WOMAN: FINDING THE WATER OF LIFE

Come, see a Man who told me all things that I ever did. Could this be the Christ?

(JOHN 4:29)

READ

READING ASSIGNMENT
Read Chapter 8 of *Twelve Extraordinary Women*.

BIBLICAL FOCUS
Key passages related to this section of the book: John 4:1–42.

REVIEW

ANOTHER LOOK
The following questions will help you review the material in Chapter 8.

1. What about the setting of the Samaritan woman's story makes it remarkable? What was distinctive about the well itself that makes it an important symbol in this story?

2. Why was it unusual for Jesus to be in Samaria?

3. Why was it unusual for Jesus to speak to this Samaritan woman or to take water from her?

4. What are the characteristics of the "living water" that Jesus offered to the Samaritan woman?

   How would you define "living water" to someone who did not know Christ?

5. What was the marital state of this woman?

   Why did Jesus call attention to the fact that she had no husband?

6. What do "true worshipers" do?

7. What did the Samaritan woman do after her conversation with Jesus?

In what ways was hers a "normal" response?

What about her response was unusual?

8. Compare how the people of Sychar responded to Jesus to the way in which various groups of Pharisees and scribes responded to Him during His earthly ministry. (Refer to Luke 15:2; Luke 19:7; and Matt. 11:19.)

BIBLE CONNECTIONS

These questions give you an opportunity to reflect on specific biblical passages associated with this lesson.

1. Read John 4:4. Can you identify a time in your life when you needed to do something that made no sense to any one else, but was nonetheless something that you knew the Lord was requiring you to do?

2. Read John 4:6–7. What do these two verses reveal to us about the nature of Jesus?

3. Read John 4:11–12. What are the short answers to the two questions the Samaritan woman asked Jesus in these verses?

4. Read Romans 5:8. How is the experience of this Samaritan woman a "foreshadow" of the truth expressed by the apostle Paul?

ADDING TO YOUR SCRIPTURAL VOCABULARY AND UNDERSTANDING

SAMARITAN: A mixed-race people descended from pagans who had intermarried with the Israelites after the Assyrians conquered the northern kingdom in 722 BC. Nehemiah wrote that a marriage between the Jewish high priest's grandson and a Samaritan girl "defiled the priesthood and the covenant of the priesthood and the Levites" (Neh. 13:29). The Samaritans had a false priesthood, a false temple, and while they regarded the first five books of the Old Testament as Scripture, they rejected the psalms and prophets.

CONSIDER: What is the balance between reaching out to people who are considered to be impure, or who might be perceived to contaminate our reputation or social cliques, and refraining from all evil and even the appearance of evil?

5. Read Ephesians 2:8–9. In what ways does the story of the Samaritan woman illustrate the truth of this passage of Scripture?

6. Read John 4:22. How does the phrase "salvation is of the Jews" address the widespread erroneous thinking that there are "many equal and acceptable paths to God"?

   In what ways was Jesus confronting false religions when He said, "You worship what you do not know; we know what we worship"?

7. Read John 4:25 and Matthew 16:17–19. How was Peter's claim about Christ related to what the Samaritan woman said?

8. Read John 10:20–25 and Mark 14:61–64. Compare these declarations of Christ with the statement Jesus made to the Samaritan woman.

9. Read John 4:40–42. Why was it important that the people of Sychar came to believe Jesus was the Christ because they had heard Him for themselves, not because of what this woman said?

HIGHLIGHTING THE LESSON

1. What is staggeringly unexpected about this whole fantastic account is that Jesus chose this time and this place and this woman to be part of the setting where He would (for the first time ever) formally and explicitly unveil His true identity as the Messiah. What does this story tell you about God's timing and methods?

2. Jesus did not offer "living water" to the Samaritan woman on the basis of anything she gave to Him or on the basis of who she was. He let her know that He knew she was a sinner and unworthy of His offer—even so He made His offer of living water to her. What a picture of God's grace and mercy! He offers us living water even when we are sinners. Why is it important that we never lose sight of this truth?

LASTING IMPLICATIONS

1. As a result of reading and studying the story of the Samaritan woman, in what ways are you feeling challenged to reach out to those who might not fit your preconceived notions about who might be the best potential converts to Christ?

2. In what ways are you feeling challenged to help those who have strong preconceived notions of what the Messiah ought to be or about what God ought to do for them?

In what ways are you feeling challenged to help those who have a wrong concept of God's nature or are serving false gods in false religions?

REFLECT AND RESPOND

DAILY ASSIGNMENT

Day One—An Outcast in an Ordinary Setting

Here is an anonymous woman who performed the most mundane of everyday tasks: she came to draw her daily ration of water for her household. She came alone, at an hour when she probably expected to find no one else at the well. (That was probably an indication of her status as an outcast.) Jesus, traveling through the region on His way to Jerusalem, was resting near the well. His disciples were purchasing food in the nearby village. Jesus, having no utensil or rope with which to draw water, asked the woman to fetch Him a drink. It was not the stuff of great drama.

She immediately expressed surprise that He would even speak to her, much less drink from her vessel. Gender taboos, racial divisions, and the class system would normally keep a man of Jesus' status from conversing with a woman such as her, much less drinking from a water container that belonged to her.

1. REFLECT: Is any person ever an outcast to Jesus?

REFLECT: Is any moment an ordinary moment in God's eyes?

RESPOND: Describe an encounter with Christ you experienced while doing mundane everyday tasks.

What did you learn from that experience?

In what ways is the Lord challenging you today to see people and tasks in a new light?

2. REFLECT: Have you ever felt prejudice from other people solely on the basis of your racial, ethnic, cultural background, or the neighborhood in which you grew up?

If so, how have you handled those feelings?

How have you responded to those who have looked down on you for factors beyond your control?

RESPOND: In what ways is the Lord challenging you regarding built-in prejudices you may have toward people of other races, ethnic or cultural backgrounds, or social status?

RESPONDING IN PRAYER

Dear Lord, help me to see that there are no ordinary moments and no outcast people from Your perspective. Help me to see the moments of my day and the chance encounters I have today as gifts from You. Help me to be Your servant at all times and to all people. In our Lord Jesus' name. Amen.

DAILY ASSIGNMENT

Day Two—An Offer of Living Water

Jesus said, "If you knew the gift of God and who it is who says to you, 'Give Me a drink,' you would have asked Him, and He would have given you living water" (John 4:10). She immediately understood that He was making an amazing claim.

1. REFLECT: Many people live on the surface, paying attention only to physical, natural experiences. Why is it important that we choose to "go deep" and pay close attention to the spiritual and eternal aspects of every situation?

   REFLECT: Have you ever had a conversation in which you thought you and another person were talking about one thing, only to discover that the other person thought you were talking about something else? If so, how did you resolve that miscommunication?

   Why is it important to make sure that communication is clear?

   RESPOND: In what ways is the Lord challenging you to be sensitive to spiritual opportunities in the ordinary conversations you have?

2. REFLECT: Jesus asked this woman for a physical drink of water and then offered to give her a spiritual, eternal drink of water. He connected with her life in order to give her His life. In what ways has Jesus connected with you?

Can you see any connections in your own life between what He asks of you and what He desires to give to you?

RESPOND: As you have reflected on what Jesus asks of you and gives to you, is there something that you feel you need to give to the Lord today in order to receive something eternal from Him? If so, what is the gift you believe the Lord desires you to make?

RESPONDING IN PRAYER

Jesus, help me to understand clearly what it is that You are asking of me and what it is that You desire to give to me. I desire to receive everything that You offer to me because I know it will be for my eternal best. Help me to give up anything of this life that You require me to give up so I might attain all that You have for me in heaven. In our Lord Jesus' name. Amen.

DAILY ASSIGNMENT

Day Three—No Husband to Call

The truth about her life was so horrible that she could not admit it to Him. No matter. He knew all about her sin right down to the infinitesimal details. Yet, far from spurning her or castigating her, He had offered her the water of life!

1. REFLECT: Why are we always challenged by the Lord to own up to our own sinfulness?

REFLECT: Why is it important that we never think that we have done anything to deserve God's gracious forgiveness and mercy?

RESPOND: Confess any sins that the Lord may be bringing to your mind and heart so that you might receive His forgiveness right now! Write out a one-sentence statement of confession.

2. REFLECT: The Samaritan woman saw her sin as a significant issue. Jesus focused on the issue of her forgiveness and the eternal life He desired to give to her. Why is it important that we focus more on what Jesus desires to do for us—cleanse us and make us whole—than on what we have done in our past?

REFLECT: What is the potential error in continually pointing to our past as we share with others our salvation testimony?

Why is it important to keep the focus on what Jesus offers and what Jesus does for us as Savior?

RESPOND: In what ways are you feeling challenged in your heart and mind as a result of reading and studying this conversation between Jesus and the Samaritan woman?

RESPONDING IN PRAYER

Heavenly Father, I know that I am a sinner in need of forgiveness. I confess to You that I have sinned. I ask You to forgive me, cleanse me, and help me to repent and move forward in the newness of life that You so generously offer to me. Help me always to be mindful that You are my Savior. Help me to follow You daily as my Lord. In our Lord Jesus' name. Amen.

DAILY ASSIGNMENT

Day Four—True Worship

Jesus said, "True worshipers will worship the Father in spirit and truth; for the Father is seeking such to worship Him. God is Spirit, and those who worship Him must worship in spirit and truth" (John 4:23–24). With that reply, He accomplished several things. First, he let her know that where you worship isn't the issue. True worshipers are defined by whom and how they worship. Second, He made it clear that the religious tradition she had grown up in was totally and utterly false.

1. REFLECT: In what ways might it be difficult for a woman to give up her religious traditions?

    REFLECT: Jesus said to the Samaritan woman, "You worship what you do not know; we know what we worship" (John 4:22). All other religions rely on speculation and mystery to cover what they "don't know" about God, heaven, or redemption. What is it that you know as a Christian about the nature of God and the salvation made available through Christ Jesus?

    RESPOND: Write out a brief statement of what you *know* to be the truth of your relationship with Jesus Christ.

2. REFLECT: The Samaritan woman expressed embryonic faith when she said she knew Messiah was coming and that "when He comes, He will tell us all things" (John 4:25). In what way was this a statement she only could have made because the Father was revealing the truth to her?

REFLECT: In what way is it only possible for us to worship the Lord in "spirit" because of what the Lord reveals to our own hearts?

RESPOND: In what ways are you feeling challenged as you read John 4:22–25?

RESPONDING IN PRAYER
Heavenly Father, show me how to worship You more fully in spirit and in truth. Help me to be keenly sensitive to what You speak to my spirit as I read and study Your Word. Help me to be confident in those things that You confirm to my heart. In our Lord Jesus' name. Amen.

DAILY ASSIGNMENT
Day Five—An Astonishing Revelation

No sooner had she broached the subject of the Messiah, than Jesus said, "I who speak to you am He" (John 4:26). This is the single most direct and explicit messianic claim Jesus ever made. Never before in any of the biblical record had He said this so forthrightly to anyone. Never again is it recorded that He declared Himself this plainly, until the night of His betrayal.

His self-revelation is a testimony to her faith. The fact that He declared Himself so plainly is proof positive that the tiny germ of hope that had her looking for the Messiah in the first place was either about to develop into authentic, full-fledged faith—or else it already had sprouted. Jesus would not have committed Himself to an unbeliever (John 2:24).

1. REFLECT: In what ways has Jesus revealed to you that He is the Christ?

   RESPOND: In what ways is the Lord challenging you today to respond to the truth that Jesus is the Christ?

2. REFLECT: The Samaritan woman's story is an example to us that Jesus responds to any degree of faith that a person may exhibit toward Him. We do not need great faith to receive Jesus as Savior—Jesus responds to even the least amount of faith with a revelation to that person's heart about who He is. In what ways does this truth bring comfort to you?

   In what ways does this truth challenge you to share the gospel more freely with others?

   REFLECT: Have you ever felt that you were missing out on a deeper relationship with Christ because you lack faith?

   RESPOND: In what ways are you feeling challenged to trust God more?

RESPONDING IN PRAYER

Dear Lord, I believe You are the Christ. I accept You as my Savior. I want to learn more about You and to know You more fully. Show me how to trust You more and more. I ask this in our Lord Jesus' name. Amen.

9

MARTHA AND MARY: WORKING AND WORSHIPING

Mary . . . sat at Jesus' feet and heard His word. But Martha was distracted with much serving.

(LUKE 10:39–40)

READ

READING ASSIGNMENT
Read Chapter 9 of *Twelve Extraordinary Women.*

BIBLICAL FOCUS
Key passages related to this section of the book: Luke 10:38–42; John 11:1–45; John 12:1–7; Matthew 26:6–13; and Mark 14:3–9.

REVIEW

ANOTHER LOOK
The following questions will help you review the material in Chapter 9.

1. How were Martha and Mary similar?

    How were they different?

2. Briefly describe the family of Martha, Mary, and Lazarus.

3. What reasons might Mary have had for anointing Jesus' feet and head with a lavish outpouring of spikenard?

    From Jesus' perspective, what did Mary's action represent?

4. In what two ways did Jesus' interaction with Mary and Martha contribute to His betrayal and arrest in Jerusalem?

5. In Luke 10:38–42, how did Martha and Mary each respond to Jesus' presence in their home?

6. Consider the different responses of Martha and Mary when Jesus arrived after Lazarus' burial. What can we learn about the inner temperament of these two women from that incident?

What does it mean to you that Jesus dealt with each woman in equally compassionate but distinctively different ways?

7. In what ways do Martha and Mary depict the contrast between doing good works and having faith?

BIBLE CONNECTIONS

These questions give you an opportunity to reflect on specific biblical passages associated with this lesson.

1. Read Romans 12:13. What does it mean to be "given to hospitality"?

How does hospitality relate to the phrase, "distributing to the needs of the saints"?

2. Read John 11:5. What happens in a person's emotions and desires when that person comes to fully accept that he or she is loved by Jesus?

3. Read Luke 10:38–42. Highlight or circle phrases or words that seem to stand out to you. Why do you think these phrases or words are important to you?

Now it happened as they went that He entered a certain village; and a certain woman named Martha welcomed Him into her house. And she had a sister called Mary, who also sat at Jesus' feet and heard His word. But Martha was distracted with much serving, and she approached Him and said, "Lord, do You not care that my sister has left me to serve alone? Therefore tell her to help me."

And Jesus answered and said to her, "Martha, Martha, you are worried and troubled about many things. But one thing is needed, and Mary has chosen that good part, which will not be taken away from her." (Luke 10:38–42)

4. Read Luke 7:36–50; John 13:1–7; and 2 John 10–11. Compare the hospitality Jesus received in Martha's house to these examples of very bad hospitality Jesus had received from other people at other times.

5. Read Luke 6:36 and Romans 14:4. In what ways was Martha judging Mary?

Why wasn't it Martha's role to judge?

HIGHLIGHTING THE LESSON

1. Jesus said that Mary had "chosen that good part" in sitting at His feet, listening to Him, rather than bustling about in meal preparation with Martha (Luke 10:42). This establishes worship as the highest of all priorities for every Christian. Nothing, including even service rendered to Christ, is more important than listening to Him and honoring Him with our hearts. What does it mean to you to "sit at the feet of Jesus" in your world today?

2. Good deeds, human charity, and acts of kindness are crucial expressions of real faith, but they must flow from a true reliance on God's redemption and His righteousness. After all, our own good works can never be a means of earning God's favor; that's why in Scripture the focus on faith is always on what God has done for us, and never on what we do for Him. How can we ensure that our good works are expressions of devotion and thanksgiving, rather than an attempt to win God's favor or make ourselves worthy in His sight?

LASTING IMPLICATIONS

1. It is a danger, even for people who love Christ, that we not become so concerned with doing things for Him that we begin to neglect hearing Him and remembering what He has done for us. We must never allow our service for Christ to crowd out our worship of Him. What can we do to ensure that we hear Christ before we embark on "doing things" in His name?

2. Martha apparently learned the lesson that Jesus asked her to learn. At the time Mary poured her costly flask of spikenard over Jesus' head and feet, Martha voiced no criticism of her sister. She was in full agreement with her act of devotion. In what ways are we challenged to grow from our mistakes and to become increasingly pure in our devotion and worship?

REFLECT AND RESPOND

DAILY ASSIGNMENT

Day One—A Ministry of Hospitality

Jesus enjoyed hospitality in the home of this family. He went there on at least three crucial occasions in the Gospels. Bethany was apparently a regular stop for Him in His travels, and this family's home seems to have become a welcome hub for Jesus during His visits to Judea.

1. REFLECT: What makes a person's home a place you like to make a regular stop on your travels?

   REFLECT: What is your definition of hospitality?

   REFLECT: What is the difference between having someone stay with you as your guest and having that person make your home a hub for his or her activities while in your area?

RESPOND: Identify several ways in which you might make your home a more welcoming place for Christian guests. (Even the most generous hostess or host can increase his or her level of hospitality.)

2. REFLECT: Read 1 Timothy 3:2; Titus 1:8; and 1 Peter 4:9. In each case "ministers" are described as people who are hospitable. How are ministry and hospitality linked?

ADDING TO YOUR SCRIPTURAL VOCABULARY AND UNDERSTANDING

ANOINT FOR BURIAL: Jesus said this about Mary's pouring a costly flask of fragrant oil over His body: "She has done what she could. She has come beforehand to anoint My body for burial" (Mark 14:8). During the first century, lavish sums were often spent on funerals, which included costly perfumes to cover the repulsive smell of decay. Bodies were loosely wrapped with strips of linen cloth. These strips were layered with spices, and additional spices were placed around the body as a whole. Hours and days after burial, additional fragrant oils were sometimes added to the cloths as necessary. Mary's anointing of Jesus was in advance of His death, not after it. There would be no need for it *after* His death—He rose from the grave before her strong-scented oil would be needed!

CONSIDER: How important is it to give our best and highest to the Lord *now*, rather than wait for some unknown time and opportunity in the future?

REFLECT: What do you believe is involved in a ministry of hospitality?

Is this ministry to be limited to other Christians?

To what degree does a person need to safeguard his or her home against forces of evil?

RESPOND: In what ways is the Lord challenging you regarding a ministry of hospitality?

RESPONDING IN PRAYER

Dear Lord, Help me to become an even wiser person in my use of the resources You have placed into my hand. Show me how I can be hospitable to others and minister to their needs through the use of my home. Show me how to safeguard my home as a haven of right-eousness, purity, spiritual comfort and encouragement, and holiness. In our Lord Jesus' name. Amen.

DAILY ASSIGNMENT

Day Two—A Costly and Meaningful Gift

Martha and Mary seemed to understand that Jesus had put Himself in jeopardy in order to give them back the life of their brother. In fact, the full depth of Mary's gratitude and understanding was revealed in a third and final account where Mary anointed the feet of Jesus with costly ointment and wiped His feet with her hair. She must have strongly suspected that her brother's resurrection would drive Jesus' enemies to a white-hot hatred, and they would be determined to put Him to death.

1. REFLECT: How do you express your gratitude to Jesus for healing you or a loved one, or for answering a prayer about something or someone very dear to your heart?

   REFLECT: Would you have made such a lavish gift to Jesus?

   If you had been Mary, would you have made such a gesture if you had known in advance the response of Judas?

   REFLECT: In what ways are we compelled to worship Christ regardless of what others may think of our acts of worship?

   RESPOND: In what way is the Lord challenging you about the ways in which you worship or give to Him?

2. REFLECT: How can we determine whether the acts of worship we make toward the Lord are truly pleasing in His sight?

REFLECT: What attributes of our heart does the Lord desire to see when we make a gift or engage in an act of worship?

RESPOND: In what way is the Lord challenging you to examine your own heart about your motives as you give to Him and worship Him?

RESPONDING IN PRAYER

Jesus, thank You for all that You have done for me and all that You are to me. Show me ways in which I might express my deep debt of gratitude toward you that truly are pleasing in Your sight. I ask this in Your name, Lord Jesus. Amen.

DAILY ASSIGNMENT

Day Three—A Great Hostess for a Great Houseguest

Martha fussed over her hostessing duties. She wanted everything to be just right. She was a conscientious and considerate hostess, and these were admirable traits. Much in her behavior was commendable.

For His part, Jesus was the perfect houseguest. He instantly made Himself at home. He enjoyed the fellowship and conversation, and as always, *His* contribution to the discussion was instructive and enlightening.

1. REFLECT: Would you have enjoyed being a guest with Martha as the hostess?

Why?

Why not?

REFLECT: What traits are required to be a good hostess?

Choose several words or phrases to describe how a good hostess behaves toward her guests?

RESPOND: In what ways do you feel challenged to reevaluate your hostessing skills?

2. REFLECT: How do you define the perfect houseguest?

REFLECT: What do you do when someone who is a guest in your home is not a good houseguest?

REFLECT: What traits are required to be a "good guest"?

Choose several words or phrases to describe how a good guest behaves toward his/her hostess?

RESPOND: In what ways do you feel challenged to be a better houseguest when you are entertained or hosted by others?

RESPONDING IN PRAYER

Heavenly Father, I acknowledge that part of having an opportunity to be a good witness of Your saving grace is to be a good hostess and also to be a good guest when I am entertained by others. Please help me to be sensitive to the needs of my guests. Please help me to be sensitive to the needs of those who host me. In our Lord Jesus' name. Amen.

DAILY ASSIGNMENT

Day Four—Two Different Responses

No doubt His disciples were asking Him questions, and He was giving answers that were thought-provoking, authoritative, and utterly edifying. Mary's instinct was to sit at His feet and listen. Martha, ever the fastidious one, went right to work with her preparations.

1. REFLECT: Would you have responded as Mary responded to the presence of Jesus in her home, or as Martha responded?

REFLECT: In what ways were Martha's feelings natural and somewhat understandable?

RESPOND: In what specific ways might the Lord be asking you to be more like Mary and less like Martha?

2. REFLECT: Did the differences in responses by Mary and Martha need to result in conflict between them?

What might have been done to avoid such a conflict?

REFLECT: Why is it important that a person not voice criticism of others in a way that detracts from a group of people serving the Lord or in a way that fosters disunity to a group of believers?

REFLECT: What are appropriate ways to express concerns about a person's laziness, unwillingness to work, or failure to pay attention to legitimate needs?

REFLECT: What errors arise when we assign motives to other people without knowing fully what their motives are?

RESPOND: In what ways is the Lord challenging you as you read about and study this conflict between Martha and Mary?

3. REFLECT: What questions do you need to ask yourself if you find yourself becoming irritated or angry with another person?

REFLECT: Identify a situation in your life, or in the life of someone close to you, in which either wrong timing or wrong priority was at the root of a conflict?

To what extent might a reevaluation of timing or priorities have helped ease the conflict?

REFLECT: Consider the possibility that nearly all conflicts can be resolved if both parties in conflict will put their focus first on worship of the Lord.

RESPOND: In what ways is the Lord challenging you to reevaluate your own conflict-resolution approaches?

RESPONDING IN PRAYER

Heavenly Father, I don't want to live in conflict with other people, but I often don't know what causes conflicts or how to resolve them. Please show me how You desire for me to behave when conflicts arise. Please show me ways in which I might avoid recurring conflicts. Please teach me how to behave in a way that lets me live in peace with others who love You as much as I do. In our Lord Jesus' name. Amen.

DAILY ASSIGNMENT

Day Five—Right in Service but Wrong in Attitude

Martha's behavior shows how subtly and sinfully human pride can corrupt even the best of our actions. What Martha was doing was by no means a bad thing. She was waiting on Christ and her other guests. In a very practical and functional sense, she was acting as servant to all, just as Christ had so often commanded. She no doubt began with the best of motives and the noblest of intentions. But the moment she stopped listening to Christ and made something other than Him the focus of her heart and attention, her perspective became very self-centered. At that point, even her service to Christ became tainted with self-absorption and spoiled by a very uncharitable failure to assume the best of her sister. Martha was showing an attitude of sinful pride that made her susceptible to several other kinds of evil as well: anger, resentment, jealousy, distrust, a critical spirit, judgmentalism, and unkindness. All of that flared up in Martha in a matter of minutes.

1. REFLECT: To what extent can good behavior be displayed even if a person has bad motives?

   To what extent can good motivations result in bad behavior?

   REFLECT: In what ways do pride and self-centeredness impact the effectiveness of our good works?

REFLECT: Pride is one of the most subtle evils. It is very difficult for a person to recognize pride in his own life, and perhaps even harder to admit it and confess it to the Lord as a sin. In an age in which strong self-esteem is advocated by so many, what are the unique challenges a person faces in discerning pride in his own heart?

RESPOND: In what ways is the Lord challenging you to evaluate your motives?

2. REFLECT: In what ways are anger, resentment, jealousy, distrust, a critical spirit, judgmentalism, or unkindness good indicators that pride is at work?

Do you perceive other indicators of pride?

RESPOND: In what ways is the Lord challenging you to confront issues related to personal pride and self-centeredness?

RESPONDING IN PRAYER
Dear Lord, I want to do the right things. I want to have the right motives. HELP ME! I ask this in Your name, Lord Jesus. Amen.

10

MARY MAGDALENE: DELIVERED FROM DARKNESS

Now when He rose early on the first day of the week, He appeared first to Mary Magdalene, out of whom He had cast seven demons.

(MARK 16:9)

READ

READING ASSIGNMENT
Read Chapter 10 of *Twelve Extraordinary Women*.

BIBLICAL FOCUS
Key passages related to this section of the book: Luke 8:1–3; Mark 16:1–10; Matt. 27:57–61; 28:1–9; Luke 24:1–12; and John 20:1–18.

REVIEW

ANOTHER LOOK
The following questions will help you review the material in Chapter 10.

1. As you have read about Mary Magdalene, what have you discovered about her that you thought you knew but truly did not know?

   What have you believed about her in the past that turned out to be accurate?

2. What symptoms of demonic possession are found in the New Testament?

   How do you define demonic possession?

   List several terms that might be used to describe the demonically possessed in the New Testament.

3. If "demon-possessed people never came to Christ to be delivered," how did Christ come into contact with them?

   How did demons respond to being in the presence of Christ Jesus?

4. What happened to Mary Magdalene after she was delivered from evil spirits?

5. While it is true that most rabbis in that culture and time did not normally allow women to be their disciples, Christ allowed women to be in His close circle of disciples. Why do we know that this was done with purity and without any hint of reproach?

6. What was unique about Mary's actions during the crucifixion and resurrection of Jesus?

BIBLE CONNECTIONS

These questions give you an opportunity to reflect on specific biblical passages associated with this lesson.

1. Read Luke 11:24–26. How would you describe the "inadequacy of self-reform" to another person?

2. Read Isaiah 64:6 and Jeremiah 13:23. What do the Scriptures say about our inability to atone for our own sins or change our own hearts?

3. Read 2 Peter 2:9 and 2 Corinthians 4:6. What is the foundation for our belief that no dominion of darkness can stand up to the light of Christ?

4. Read Matthew 11:29–30. How did Mary Magdalene typify the response Jesus desired from His disciples?

In what ways might you take Christ's "yoke" upon you and learn more of Him?

5. Read John 20:1–13. Circle or highlight any words or phrases that seem to stand out to you. Why are these words or phrases important to you?

Now on the first day of the week Mary Magdalene went to the tomb early, while it was still dark, and saw that the stone had been taken away from the tomb. Then she ran and came to Simon Peter, and to the other disciple, whom Jesus loved, and said to them, "They have taken away the Lord out of the tomb, and we do not know where they have laid Him."

Peter therefore went out, and the other disciple, and were going to the tomb. So they both ran together, and the other disciple outran Peter and came to the tomb first. And he, stooping down and looking in, saw the linen cloths lying there; yet he did not go in. Then Simon Peter came, following him, and went into the tomb; and he saw the linen cloths lying there, and the handkerchief that had been around His head, not lying with the linen cloths, but folded together in a place by itself. Then the other disciple, who came to the tomb first, went in also; and he saw and believed. For as yet they did not know the Scripture, that He must rise again from the dead. Then the disciples went away again to their own homes.

But Mary stood outside by the tomb weeping, and as she wept she stooped down and looked into the tomb. And she saw two angels in white sitting, one at the head and the other at the feet, where the body of Jesus had lain. Then they said to her, "Woman, why are you weeping"?

She said to them, "Because they have taken away my Lord, and I do not know where they have laid Him." (John 20:1–13)

6. Read John 10:3–4. How did Mary manifest the truth of these verses?

HIGHLIGHTING THE LESSON

1. Mary Magdalene knew the darkness of her own past and the way in which Jesus had brought her to a glorious bright and shining day of deliverance. She also knew the darkness of the cross and the glorious dawning of a new day at the resurrection. In what ways does Jesus always dispel the darkness of sin and its guilt, shame, and torment with the light of His love and truth?

2. Mary Magdalene was the first to see Jesus after He was risen. In what ways was she uniquely qualified for this honor?

How are we challenged as believers today to be so faithful in our devotion and love that we are the first to recognize Jesus in the midst of any situation or circumstance?

LASTING IMPLICATIONS

1. In a world in which many people need to be coaxed to come to Christ and to draw close to Him, Mary did not want to let go. What can we learn from her life?

In what ways are we challenged never to let go of Christ?

ADDING TO YOUR SCRIPTURAL VOCABULARY AND UNDERSTANDING

DISCIPLE: A disciple is literally a person who receives instruction from another person. Unlike an average student, a disciple in Jesus' time learned from a master teacher by living in close proximity to the teacher. That way, a disciple learned not only what a teacher said, but saw how a teacher applied his own teachings to real-life situations. Disciples not only learned concepts but application of concepts. The disciples of Jesus were those who walked and talked with Him on a day-in, day-out basis—learning from not only what He said and did, but how He spoke, when He acted, and the methods of application He used in dealing with various people and situations.

CONSIDER: How critical is it to know not only what Jesus said, but to know how Jesus portrayed His own teachings in deeds—including His miracles of healing and deliverance? Since Jesus is not alive on the earth today in physical form, how are we to be His disciples?

2. In a world filled with hesitation and pessimism about serving Jesus Christ, what are the lessons from Mary Magdalene's story that inspire us to respond to Him without hesitation and with great optimism and joy?

REFLECT AND RESPOND

DAILY ASSIGNMENT

Day One—Woman with a "Dark Past"

Mary Magdalene did have a dark past. Nothing indicates that her conduct was ever lewd or sordid in any way that would justify the common association of her name with sins of immorality. But Mary was indeed a woman whom Christ had liberated from demonic bondage. She is described as a woman "out of whom had come seven demons" (Luke 8:2). Mary was from the village of Magdala, which seemed to be a hotbed of demonic activity. None of the demonized individuals in the New Testament is explicitly associated with immoral behavior. Most of them were regarded as outcasts and pariahs by polite society. Scripture invariably presents them to us as victims with utterly ruined lives.

1. REFLECT: How does the place in which a person grows up make that person more susceptible to certain types of sin or evil influence?

   REFLECT: How might a person who is identified publicly as having a dark past overcome that past?

   RESPOND: As you have reflected upon these questions, how has the Lord been speaking to your heart and mind?

2. REFLECT: To what extent do we readily extend forgiveness and open arms of reconciliation to those we have heard were once demonized but are now set free?

REFLECT: Why do people usually ostracize those who are demonized?

Do we tend to treat people who previously were demonized any differently than we treat those who are presently demonized?

REFLECT: Why are we frightened by those who manifest symptoms of demonic possession?

RESPOND: As you have reflected on the questions above, how has the Lord been speaking to your heart and mind?

RESPONDING IN PRAYER
Dear Lord, I don't want to be afraid of those who have had a dark past or who are under the influence of evil today. Help me to overcome my fears and prejudices. Help me to treat people as You treated them. Help me to love people as You love them. Give me courage! In our Lord Jesus' name. Amen.

DAILY ASSIGNMENT
Day Two—A Woman Once Tormented
Satan tormented her with seven demons. There was nothing any mere man or woman

could do for her. She was a veritable prisoner of demonic affliction. These undoubtedly included depression, anxiety, unhappiness, loneliness, self-loathing, shame, fear, and a host of other similar miseries. In all probability, she suffered even worse torments, too, such as blindness, deafness, insanity, or any of the other disorders commonly associated with victims of demonic possession described in the New Testament. Whatever her condition, she would have been in perpetual agony—at least seven kinds of agony. Demoniacs in Scripture were always friendless, except in rare cases when devoted family members cared for them. They were perpetually restless, because of their inability to escape the constant torments of their demonic captors. They were continually joyless, because all of life had become darkness and misery for them. And they were hopeless, because there was no earthly remedy for their spiritual afflictions.

1. REFLECT: In what way is every believer "tormented" prior to accepting Jesus as his or her Savior?

   In what way does sin always create agony?

   REFLECT: Many people who are not demonized are nevertheless joyless, unhappy, depressed, and filled with shame and fear. Others are perpetually restless or without hope. How are we as Christians to befriend those who are living with these kinds of agony?

   REFLECT: How are we to treat Christians who seem trapped in darkness and misery? (Remember that demonization is not a sin per se, but an affliction that renders a person victimized beyond his or her control.)

Do we treat Christians who are in agony any differently than non-Christians?

RESPOND: As you have reflected on the questions above, in what ways have you felt challenged by the Lord?

2. REFLECT: How do you deal with personal times of sadness, fear, unhappiness, or anxiety?

REFLECT: How do you deal with situations that make you feel personally hopeless or discouraged?

REFLECT: In what ways is the Lord challenging you to trust Him in such times and situations?

RESPONDING IN PRAYER

Jesus, I know without a shadow of doubt that You do not desire for me to live with agony or torment for any reason or at any time. You do not desire for me to be bound by fear, discouragement, anxiety, or feelings of hopelessness. I ask You to give me the joy, peace, and hope that only You can impart to me. I ask You to deliver me from the Evil One! I pray this in Your name, Lord Jesus. Amen.

DAILY ASSIGNMENT

Day Three—A Woman Delivered

Christ had delivered her from all that. Luke and Mark seem to mention her former demonization only for the purpose of celebrating Christ's goodness and grace toward her. Perhaps she had tried to reform her own life and learned the hard way how utterly futile it is to try to free oneself from Satan's grip. Good works and religion don't atone for sin (Isa. 64:6), and no sinner has it within his power to change his own heart (Jer. 13:23).

1. REFLECT: Why is it always more important to focus on what Christ does, can do, and promises to do rather than upon the sordid details of a person's sinful past?

   REFLECT: What would you say to a person whom you perceive is relying upon religion and good works to atone for sin?

   RESPOND: As you have reflected upon the questions above, has the Lord brought a particular person to your mind and heart? If so, what do you believe the Lord desires for you to do?

2. REFLECT: Have you ever tried to reform yourself or free yourself from Satan's grip apart from Christ? If so, what were the results?

   REFLECT: What is the difference between "growth and change for the better" and "atonement and change of heart"?

Why are we wise to grow and change those things that are in our power to change?

Why are we wise to trust God alone to atone for our sins and change our hearts?

REFLECT: Why are we wise always to ask God to help us grow and change as He desires for us to grow and change?

RESPOND: As you have reflected upon the questions above, how has the Lord been dealing with you regarding your own spiritual growth and development?

RESPONDING IN PRAYER

Heavenly Father, I know that only You can atone for sin and change the human heart. Help me to trust You to do that work in me and in my loved ones. Show me how You desire for me to grow and change. Help me never to trust in anything or anyone to be my Savior apart from You. In our Lord Jesus' name. Amen.

DAILY ASSIGNMENT

Day Four—A Disciple of Jesus

Mary Magdalene joined the close circle of disciples who traveled with Jesus on His long journeys. Luke said Mary Magdalene and the other women were among many who "provided for Him from their substance" (Luke 8:3). The fact that her name appears at the head of the list of this band of women seems to indicate that she had a special place of respect among them.

Mary Magdalene remained Jesus' faithful disciple even when others forsook Him.

She first appeared in Luke's Gospel at a time when opposition to Jesus had grown to the point that He began to teach in parables (Matt. 11:10–11). When others became offended with His sayings, she stayed by His side. When others walked no longer with Him, she remained faithful.

1. REFLECT: Why do you believe Mary left Magdala and joined the close circle of disciples?

   REFLECT: In what ways would Mary's presence among the close circle of disciples have been a source of encouragement to the disciples?

   To those who came to hear Jesus preach and teach?

   REFLECT: In what ways are you a disciple of Jesus today?

   Do you believe non-Christians would identify you as part of Jesus' close circle of disciples? Why or why not?

   RESPOND: In what way is the Lord challenging you to become identified as being part of His close circle of disciples?

2. REFLECT: What does the phrase "provided for Him from their substance" mean to you?

RESPOND: In what way is the Lord challenging you today to provide for Him from your substance?

3. REFLECT: Why is it sometimes difficult to remain loyal even to a godly person who is being publicly defamed without just cause?

REFLECT: Why is it that we are so often more concerned about our reputations in association with Christ than about what Jesus thinks?

RESPOND: In what way is the Lord challenging you to become more loyal to Him and steadfast in your witness of Him?

RESPONDING IN PRAYER

Heavenly Father, I want to be a faithful, steadfast, loyal follower of Jesus. I want to be in the inner circle of His disciples on the earth today. Lead me and guide me in ways that will draw me closer to Christ so that I might take His yoke upon my life and learn more of Him. In our Lord Jesus' name. Amen.

DAILY ASSIGNMENT

Day Five—A Woman at the Cross and the Empty Tomb

Mary Magdalene was present at the crucifixion. She remained until the bitter end. There was nothing for her to do but watch and pray and grieve.

She and Mary, the Mother of James, secretly followed Joseph of Arimathea to the tomb and observed where He was laid (Mark 15:47). It must have broken her heart to see His lifeless, mangled body so poorly prepared and laid in a cold tomb. She was determined to wash and anoint His body properly.

The women went inside the sepulcher and found it empty. Mary's first inclination was to assume that someone had stolen Jesus' body. After Peter and John left the empty tomb, Mary Magdalene remained outside the tomb alone. She then stooped in and saw angels. Later, in the garden, she saw Jesus. At first, through her tear-filled eyes, she did not recognize Him.

1. REFLECT: What emotions did Mary Magdalene likely feel as she watched Jesus die on the cross?

    REFLECT: What do you believe drove Mary to follow Joseph to the tomb to see where Jesus was buried—an act that may have been very dangerous to her personally?

    REFLECT: What compelled Mary to go to the tomb before dawn on the first day of the week?

    RESPOND: In what ways have you found yourself relating to Mary as you have reflected upon the questions above?

Are there ways in which you believe you would have responded differently? If so, how?

Why?

Are there ways in which you believe the Lord is challenging you to be more like Mary?

2. REFLECT: Mary Magdalene had no thought of resurrection when she went to the tomb. She believed Jesus to be irreversibly dead. What are the emotions associated with believing that a person has died?

What are the emotions associated with believing that a relationship has died?

What are the emotions associated with believing that a dream or a hope for the future has died?

Which emotions are common to all three types of loss?

REFLECT: What is God's answer to grief of all types?

RESPOND: As you have reflected on the questions above, how has the Lord spoken to your heart and mind?

3. REFLECT: What emotions did Mary likely experience as she made her way in darkness to the tomb, experienced a great earthquake, found the tomb to be empty, saw and heard angels, saw and heard Jesus call her by name, and then heard Jesus tell her not to cling to Him but go and give instructions to His disciples?

REFLECT: Can you recall a time when you felt as if you were on an emotional roller-coaster?

How did you respond?

REFLECT: In what ways does Jesus call us to live according to the truth of His Word and not according to our own emotions in the moment?

REFLECT: Why was it important that Mary hear Jesus call her by name?

RESPOND: As you have reflected upon the questions above, in what ways has the Lord been challenging you personally to respond to Him with faith, not emotions?

RESPONDING IN PRAYER

Dear Lord, help me to trust in You regardless of the circumstances I see all around me. Help me to rely totally upon Your Word. Help me to respond to You at all times and in all situations, relationships, and experiences with devotion, love, and faith. I ask this in our Lord Jesus' name. Amen.

11

LYDIA: A HOSPITABLE HEART OPENED

Now a certain woman named Lydia heard us. She was a seller of purple from the city of Thyatria, who worshiped God. The Lord opened her heart to heed the things spoken by Paul.

(ACTS 16:14)

READ

READING ASSIGNMENT
Read Chapter 11 of *Twelve Extraordinary Women.*

BIBLICAL FOCUS
Key passages related to this section of the book: Acts 16:11–15 and Acts 16:40.

REVIEW

ANOTHER LOOK
The following questions will help you review the material in the book.

1. How would you describe Lydia to a friend who had never read about her in the Bible?

   What irony is there in her being the first Christian convert in Europe?

2. How might Lydia have concluded that the apostle Paul had been sent to Philippi just for her to come to know Christ?

ADDING TO YOUR SCRIPTURAL VOCABULARY AND UNDERSTANDING

CHURCH: The word "church" is the translation of a Greek word, *ecclesia*, which means "an assembly." A church is not a building, per se, but a body of believers in Christ Jesus. That is why we can say the church at Philippi met at Lydia's house. Her house was not "the church," but rather the meeting place for the church. The word became widely used in the New Testament times to denote local congregations of Christian believers in Jerusalem, Antioch, Ephesus, Corinth, Rome, and in various places of Asia. The word church is also used to denote the entire assembly of Christian believers worldwide.

CONSIDER: Why is it important for us never to lose sight of the fact that the church is not a building, but rather people who call Jesus their Savior and Lord?

As you recall the circumstances surrounding your own conversion, do you have a sense that God was working behind the scenes all along to bring you to that precise time and place where you might respond to the gospel and receive Jesus Christ as your Savior?

3. In what ways was Lydia an ideal person with whom someone like Paul might share the gospel?

4. What does the term irresistible grace mean to you? How did Lydia respond to God's irresistible grace?

BIBLE CONNECTIONS

These questions give you an opportunity to reflect on specific biblical passages associated with this lesson.

1. Read Romans 8:28–29. How are these verses manifested in the life of Lydia?

2. Read Proverbs 31:13, 19, 21–22. In what ways was Lydia like the woman described in Proverbs 31?

3. Read John 6:44–45. How is Lydia's story related to these words of Jesus?

4. Read Acts 16:14 and Romans 12:3. In what ways did God open Lydia's heart and ears to the truth?

   How did He open your heart and ears to the truth of the gospel and your need of a Savior?

5. Read Acts 16:15 and Acts 8:36–38. How is Lydia's story somewhat parallel to that of Philip and the Ethiopian eunuch?

   Was it any accident that both of them were close to bodies of water for baptism at the time they received Christ?

6. Read Acts 16:16–39. A slave girl who had been possessed with a spirit of divination was delivered when Paul commanded the spirit to come out of her. That act of deliverance resulted in Paul and Silas being put in the prison at Philippi. An earthquake set them free of their bonds but they remained in the

prison to witness to the jailer. The jailer and his entire family came to know Christ. How do you respond to the idea that this delivered slave girl and the jailer and his family very likely became associated with the church in Philippi?

In what ways was the church in Philippi marked by great diversity? By great unity?

7. Review the book of Philippians in the New Testament. Keep in mind that this letter from Paul was likely sent to and read within the confines of Lydia's home. What might you conclude about the ways in which the church in Lydia's house had flourished and grown in faith?

HIGHLIGHTING THE LESSON

1. Wherever you see a soul like Lydia's truly seeking God, you can be certain God is drawing her. Whenever someone trusts Christ, it is God who opens the heart to believe. If God Himself did not draw us to Christ, we would never come at all. What encouragement do you draw from this truth?

2. Lydia knew in her heart that her salvation was wholly and completely the work of God's grace. What about Lydia's story is most encouraging to you?

LASTING IMPLICATIONS

1. Lydia's story reminds us, that while God's sovereign purposes usually remain hidden from our eyes, He is always at work in secret and surprising ways to call out a people for His name. What implications does this truth have regarding your life today?

   What implications does this truth have for those with whom you might share the gospel?

2. Lydia acted immediately on her confession of faith. She was baptized, led her household to repentance, and extended hospitality to the missionary team that had shared the gospel with her. In turn, her home became the location for the earliest known church body established in Europe. What might the Lord do through your life?

REFLECT AND RESPOND

DAILY ASSIGNMENT

Day One—A Business Woman

Lydia was from Asia Minor, from the city of Thyatira—a city famous for the art of dying textiles. She was living and working in Philippi, a thriving, busy community at the crossroads of two trade routes. She sold purple dye and fancy purple cloth, manufactured by a famous guild in her hometown of Thyatira. Tyrian dye was the basis for royal purple, and that substance was one of the most precious of all commodities in the ancient world. So Lydia must have been a woman of some means, likely a wealthy woman.

1. REFLECT: Identify several ways in which you perceive God might use a Christian woman who is willing to use her business for the spread of the gospel?

   REFLECT: In what ways might God use a wealthy woman to spread the gospel?

   RESPOND: In what way is the Lord challenging you to make your talents and your financial resources available for spreading the gospel?

2. REFLECT: What potential for sharing the gospel do you see in the fact that Lydia's business was being conducted at the crossroads of two trade routes?

   REFLECT: In what ways might God use a well-connected woman to spread the gospel?

   RESPOND: In what way is the Lord challenging you to use your connections to share the gospel of Jesus Christ?

RESPONDING IN PRAYER

Dear Lord, I am willing to be used by You in whatever ways You desire to use my talents, my connections, and my resources. If there is a business or job that you want me to under-take as a means of sharing Your gospel with others, show me what to do, to whom I should speak, and when I should act. In our Lord Jesus' name. Amen.

DAILY ASSIGNMENT

Day Two—In Prayer by the River

Philippi was a thoroughly Gentile town. There were a few Jews in Philippi, but very few—not even enough to support a synagogue. In communities without synagogues, Jewish women could pray together in groups if they liked, but men had to form a legitimate *minyan* (a group of ten Jewish men deemed to be a quorum for establishing a synagogue) before they could partake in any kind of formal, public, communal worship—including prayer, the reading of the Torah, or the giving of public blessings.

1. REFLECT: What does the fact that Lydia was praying at the river tell us about Lydia's spiritual nature?

    REFLECT: Why is it important that Christian women gather to pray for others?

    In what ways might a Christian woman have greater sensitivity and empathy than a Christian man for a woman in need?

    How might a woman's intuition, emotions, sensitivity, and ability to empathize be used in a powerful way in prayer?

RESPOND: As you have reflected upon the questions above, in what ways has the Lord been speaking to your heart and mind?

2. REFLECT: Lydia, as a Gentile, was giving up what would have been a normal business day to meet together with Jewish women to pray. What does this tell you about the priority that Lydia had placed upon getting to know God better?

REFLECT: What do people who are interested in knowing more about God tend to do in pursuit of that interest?

What priorities in a person's life are likely to change when a person begins to actively seek to know God, or to know Him better?

RESPOND: In what way is the Lord challenging you as you reflect upon the questions above?

RESPONDING IN PRAYER

Jesus, show me the people around me who are most ready to hear about You and receive You into their lives. Teach me what I might say to them about You. Give me the courage to go to them and share the gospel. I pray this in Your name, Lord Jesus. Amen.

DAILY ASSIGNMENT

Day Three—An Active Seeker of the True God

Lydia was a Gentile, an active seeker of the true God who had not yet become a formal Jewish proselyte (Acts 16:14). Luke says that Lydia "heard us" (Acts 16:14).

1. REFLECT: What does the phrase "active seeker of the true God" mean to you?

How might a person discern that another human being is an "active seeker of the true God"? How important is it that we discern those within our sphere of influence who might be "active seekers of the true God" and focus our sharing of the gospel on them?

REFLECT: As you have reflected on the questions above, has the Lord brought particular individuals, a family, or group of people to your heart and mind?

How do you believe the Lord wants you to reach out to them with the gospel?

2. REFLECT: What does it mean to you that Lydia "heard" Paul and others on his missionary team? What is the difference between "overhearing" or "casually hearing," and actively, intently, and intentionally "hearing"?

RESPOND: In what ways do you desire to be more active, intentional, and intent on hearing more about the Lord?

RESPONDING IN PRAYER

Heavenly Father, I want to know everything I can possibly know about You. I want to know more about what You desire to do in my life and through my life to reach others. Teach me, Lord! Show me the paths in which You desire that I walk. Help me to hear You with spiritual ears and not to miss a word that You speak to my heart. In our Lord Jesus' name. Amen.

DAILY ASSIGNMENT

Day Four—Her Household Was Baptized with Her

Luke writes, "And when she and her household were baptized. . ." (Acts 16:15). Her "household" might describe her actual family or her servants. But whoever was included in the household, they all came to faith and were baptized right along with Lydia. She was already leading others to Christ. And God was graciously opening their hearts too.

1. REFLECT: What seems to make one person's conversion to Christ or one person's desire to know the Lord infectious?

   What are the qualities in newly converted people that seem to open the hearts of others around them to accept the Lord?

   RESPOND: In what way is the Lord encouraging you today to share the gospel with those in your immediate family who do not know Christ, or to share the gospel with those who are employed by you?

2. REFLECT: What is the importance of baptism after a person has accepted Jesus as Savior?

REFLECT: Describe your own baptism and its importance in your life?

RESPOND: As you have reflected upon the questions above, how has the Lord been speaking to your heart and mind?

RESPONDING IN PRAYER

Heavenly Father, give me a joy in my salvation that is infectious! Help me to reach out to my family members and those who work alongside me with renewed enthusiasm, sensitivity, and joy. Show me how best to share the gospel with them. In our Lord Jesus' name. Amen.

DAILY ASSIGNMENT

Day Five—Hospitality and the Founding of a Church

Luke said that Lydia begged Paul and his team to be her guests—and she persuaded them to do so. Paul's team included Silas, Timothy, Luke, and perhaps others. It would be no easy task, even today, to host so many strangers. Since they had no plans for where to go next (they were there, after all, to plant a church), she was offering to keep them indefinitely. In extending hospitality to Paul and his missionary team, she was exposing herself to possible trouble—a loss of business, bad will in the community, and even a prison sentence for herself.

1. REFLECT: Paul and Silas were ultimately beaten badly, thrown in jail, and clamped in stocks for preaching the gospel in Philippi. If preaching the gospel was deemed a jailable offense, Lydia was also exposing herself to possible

trouble. In what ways does Lydia's hospitality seem courageous and bold in light of the potential consequences?

REFLECT: In what ways does alignment with a group of missionary-minded Christians have the potential to impact a person's business, their reputation in the community, and even their standing before the law (especially in some nations around the world)?

Should a person evaluate these potential consequences in determining whether to extend hospitality?

If so, what should be considered?

RESPOND: As you have reflected upon the questions above, how has the Lord been speaking to your heart and mind?

2. REFLECT: Why was Lydia likely eager to have Paul and his team in her home?

In what ways do you long to spend time with those who are more mature than you in their faith, or who know more about the Scripture than you know?

REFLECT: Are you willing to use your home as a place of discipleship and worship?

Why or why not?

REFLECT: After their release from prison, Paul and Silas returned to Lydia's house to encourage the brethren before they departed. How might one establish his or her home as a place where fellow believers are encouraged in their faith and thus, made bolder witnesses?

RESPOND: In what ways might the Lord be challenging you to reach out to someone and extend hospitality to that person?

In what ways might the Lord be challenging you to use your home or place of business as a meeting place for Christians?

RESPONDING IN PRAYER

Dear Lord, I want to have the courage to make available to You all of my life and all of my resources, for whatever tasks or ministry of hospitality that you might ask of me. Help me to love You more fully, with a heart open to others and hands willing to give. Show me ways in which my home might be a place where other Christians are encouraged in spirit and made more bold to share the gospel with lost souls. I ask this in our Lord Jesus' name. Amen.

12

GOD'S WOMEN:
NOBLE AND INFLUENTIAL

We all, with unveiled face, beholding as in a mirror the glory of the Lord, are being transformed into the same image from glory to glory, just as by the Spirit of the Lord.

(2 COR. 3:18)

READ

READING ASSIGNMENT

Read the Epilogue and reread the Introduction of *Twelve Extraordinary Women*. In addition, review the overall contents of the book and what you have written in this workbook.

BIBLICAL FOCUS

Key passages related to this section of the book: 2 Corinthians 3:18 and Proverbs 31:10–30.

REVIEW

ANOTHER LOOK

The following questions will help you review the material you have studied.

1. Briefly summarize the key spiritual traits or moral virtues that you associate with each woman covered in this study.

Eve

Sarah

Rahab

Ruth

Hannah

Mary, the mother of Jesus

Anna

Samaritan woman

Martha and Mary

Mary Magdalene

Lydia

2. From the very first chapter of the Bible, we are taught that women, like men, bear the stamp of God's own image. In what ways do these women, taken as a whole, bear the stamp of God's own image?

3. In the social and religious life of Israel and the New Testament church, women were never relegated to the background. In what specific ways did women participate fully in the life and worship of God's people?

4. How did Jesus include or treat women?

BIBLE CONNECTIONS

These questions give you an opportunity to reflect on specific biblical passages associated with this lesson.

1. Read 2 Corinthians 4:7. How does this verse apply to the women whose lives were studied in this book?

   In what way do you personally take comfort in this verse?

2. Read Luke 19:10 and Mark 2:17. How do these words of Jesus apply to the women whose lives were studied in this book?

   In what ways do these words of Jesus encourage you?

3. Read 2 Corinthians 3:18. How does this verse apply to the women whose lives were studied in this book?

In what ways do you see this verse applying to your own life?

HIGHLIGHTING THE LESSON

1. Everything that made these women extraordinary was ultimately owing to the work of the glorious Savior whom they loved and served. God was the truly extraordinary One, and He was simply conforming these women to their Savior's likeness. Extraordinary as they seem, what God was doing in their lives is really no different from what He does in the life of every true believer. How is the work that the Lord ultimately did in each of these women's lives being accomplished in your life?

ADDING TO YOUR SCRIPTURAL VOCABULARY AND UNDERSTANDING

GLORY OF THE LORD: This phrase refers to the one-of-a-kind and absolute perfection of *all* the divine attributes taken as a whole. In the New Testament, the concept "from glory to glory" refers to a continual progressive transformation of a believer from spiritual immaturity and a life prone to character flaws and failures into spiritual maturity and Christ-likeness. As the believer continually focuses on Christ Jesus, the Spirit does the transforming work. The phrase describes a progressive sanctification—the more believers grow in their knowledge of Christ, the more He is revealed in their lives.

CONSIDER: Why must we trust the Spirit to do a transformative work in us, rather than seek to glorify ourselves?

2. Godliness and good works are the real essence of feminine beauty. That truth is exemplified to one degree or another by every woman featured in this book. In what ways have you been challenged by this study to place greater emphasis on godliness and good works in your life?

LASTING IMPLICATIONS

1. Scripture never discounts the female intellect, downplays the talents and abilities of women, or discourages the right use of women's spiritual gifts. But whenever the Bible expressly talks about the marks of an excellent woman, the stress is always on feminine virtue. The most significant women in Scripture were influential not because of their careers, but because of their character. In what ways has this study challenged you to place greater emphasis in your life upon virtue and character?

2. The faithfulness of these women is their true, lasting legacy. In what ways has this study challenged you to be more faithful to the Lord Jesus Christ?

REFLECT AND RESPOND

DAILY ASSIGNMENT
Day One—God's Woman Is Christ-Centered
The faith and hope of these women was absolutely and resolutely Christ-centered. That is the single, central, dominant truth that emerges from a study of all the godly women in Scripture.

1. REFLECT: What does it mean for your life to be Christ-centered?

   RESPOND: What practical and specific things might you do to make your life more Christ-centered?

   In what ways might you teach other women or girls to be Christ-centered?

2. How can a woman ensure that her faith is absolutely and resolutely Christ-centered?

   REFLECT: How can a woman ensure that her hopes are absolutely and resolutely Christ-centered?

   RESPOND: In what way is the Lord speaking to your heart about focusing your faith and hopes on Christ Jesus?

RESPONDING IN PRAYER
Dear Lord, I place all of my faith and hope in You. Help me to make every choice and decision in my life today with You at the forefront of my thinking and with You at the center of my heart. In our Lord Jesus' name. Amen.

DAILY ASSIGNMENT

Day Two—Character and Feminine Virtue

The women whose lives we have been studying aren't memorable solely because of their physical beauty, their natural abilities, their personal accomplishments, or some position they attained. They aren't distinguished for any of the typical reasons celebrity is conferred on certain women these days. Most of them did not marry into any kind of fame or influence. The fruit of their faith was virtue. The accounts of each of them illustrate, in some significant way, a particular moral quality or spiritual trait that is worthy of emulation.

1. REFLECT: What does the phrase "fruit of their faith was virtue" mean to you?

   RESPOND: In what way is the Lord challenging you to exhibit your faith through virtuous character and deeds?

2. REFLECT: As you have studied these twelve women, is there one who stood out to you as embodying a particular moral quality or spiritual trait that you desire to establish in your life?

   How might a person go about developing such a quality or trait?

   REFLECT: Which of these women would you most like to emulate, and why?

RESPOND: Identify one or two very practical and specific steps you can take to help develop greater virtue and spiritual maturity.

RESPONDING IN PRAYER

Jesus, teach me how I might become a more virtuous person. Show me how to develop increasingly into character that You displayed on this earth. Show me how to grow spiritually into Your likeness. I pray this in Your name, Lord Jesus. Amen.

DAILY ASSIGNMENT

Day Three—Imperfect Vessels Used by God

Not one of those women was perfect, of course. Their flaws and failures are evident, too, and those are also recorded for our admonition. Such stories also comfort us with the reminder that throughout history, God has used imperfect vessels.

1. REFLECT: In what ways do we allow our flaws and failures to keep us from seeking to know the Lord at a deeper level?

    RESPOND: What do you believe the Lord desires for you when it comes to His relationship with you?

    What might you do to develop a deeper relationship with Christ?

2. REFLECT: In what ways do we often allow our flaws and failures to keep us from volunteering for active ministry or outreach roles?

RESPOND: How is the Lord speaking to your heart about becoming more involved in ministry to other people?

RESPONDING IN PRAYER

Heavenly Father, help me to fully accept Your forgiveness and to fully receive Your love, Your approval, and the worth that You give to my life. Help me to fully use all of the talents and abilities You have given to me for Your sake and to bring glory to You. In our Lord Jesus' name. Amen.

DAILY ASSIGNMENT

Day Four—The Gospel that Elevates

Wherever the gospel has spread, the social, legal, and spiritual status of women has, as a rule, been elevated. When the gospel has been eclipsed (whether by repression, false religion, secularism, humanistic philosophy, or spiritual decay within the church), the status of women has declined accordingly.

1. REFLECT: Cite a specific example in which you believe women have been elevated socially, legally, or spiritually because of the gospel?

REFLECT: In what ways is the spreading of the gospel the most effective thing you might do to improve the lives of women who are currently being persecuted or "put down" by their prevailing culture?

RESPOND: As you have reflected upon the questions above, how has the Lord been speaking to your heart and mind?

2. REFLECT: Are there specific examples in your life in which you see repression, false religion, secularism, humanistic philosophy, or spiritual decay within the church at work?

What are the effects?

RESPOND: In what way is the Lord challenging you to confront the eclipse of the gospel?

RESPONDING IN PRAYER
Heavenly Father, show me specific ways in which I might do more to extend the gospel to my culture and around the world. In our Lord Jesus' name. Amen.

DAILY ASSIGNMENT
Day Five—Exalted for All the Right Reasons
One of the unique features of the Bible is the way it exalts women. Scripture often seems to go out of the way to pay homage to them, to ennoble their roles in society and family, to acknowledge the importance of their influence, and to exalt the virtues of women who were particularly godly examples.

Women are by no means marginalized or relegated to any second-class status (Gal. 3:28). The Bible acknowledges and celebrates the priceless value of a virtuous woman (Prov. 12:4, 31:10; 1 Cor. 11:7).

1. REFLECT: Do you exalt the role of women as much as the Bible does?

Why or why not?

Do you believe others around you exalt the role of women?

REFLECT: Have you ever personally felt marginalized or relegated to second-class status?

How did you respond?

How did you wish you had responded?

RESPOND: As you have reflected on the questions above, how has the Lord been challenging you to see women as He sees them?

2. REFLECT: In what ways is a virtuous woman priceless?

RESPOND: How might you do more to acknowledge and celebrate the price-less value of virtue?

RESPONDING IN PRAYER
Dear Lord, help me to see women as You see them. Help me to treat women as You treat them. Help me to see myself and treat myself as You see me. I ask this in our Lord Jesus' name. Amen.

LEADER'S NOTES

CHAPTER 1

1. These may be among the terms used to describe Eve: unsurpassed beauty; crown and pinnacle of God's amazing creative work; first female; carefully designed from living flesh and bone; glorious refinement of humanity; a gift to Adam; necessary partner to Adam; only human being ever directly created by God from living tissue; flawless; unsurpassed charm, grace, virtue, ingenuity, and wit; great intelligence; pure innocence; strong; beautiful; radiant; carefully constructed and designed.

   DISCUSS: Are these the attributes we have today for female perfection in our culture? In the church?

2. We know these things about Eve: her name (used only four times in Scripture: Gen. 3:20; 4:1; 2 Cor. 11:3; 1 Tim. 2:13), her description as the "mother of all living," the way in which she was created, her temptation and fall, the curse placed on her, that she bore Cain, Abel, and Seth, and the hope to which she clung. Among the things we don't know about Eve: her physical description, how many children she had, how long she lived, and where and how she died.

   DISCUSS: To what extent do we tend to focus on physical and outer attributes and facts rather than the spiritual or inner attributes of a person?

   Where does "relationship" identity fit into a woman's description—for example, the identity that might be drawn from the words "sister," "wife," "mother," "grandmother," "friend"?

3. Four lessons drawn from the way in which Eve was created: 1) her fundamental equality with Adam (of same essential nature); 2) the essential unity of the ideal marriage relationship; 3) the deep and meaningful aspects of marriage that are beyond physical union (union of heart and soul); and, 4) insights into the divinely-designed role for women as fulfilling a different function.

   DISCUSS: Which of these four lessons is most intriguing or challenging to you and why?

4. Satan's *modus operandi* in temptation: 1) come in disguise; 2) come when a person is most vulnerable; 3) question the Word of God (raise doubt about its truthfulness, question truthfulness of Word, insinuate suspicion about God's motives, voice apprehension about God's wisdom); 4) twist or misquote the Word of God; and, 5) ultimately directly refute the Word of God and substitute another version of consequences associated with God's commandments.

   DISCUSS: Genesis 3:4–5. The serpent promised Eve: You will not die, your eyes will be opened, you will be like God, you will know good and evil. In what ways does Satan promise us these things today? How enticing are the human desires to live forever, understand all mysteries, have the power and glory of God, and have a full knowledge of both good and evil? Why are these things impossible for a finite human being? Why do they *appear* to be good things?

5. Some of the ways in which people respond to their sins are: fear, hiding from God, sorrow, and blame-shifting. People also diminish the seriousness of their sin through self-justification through comparison to others, self-betterment schemes, and blaming God for "making a person" prone to a particular type of sin.

   DISCUSS: Why are each of these attempts to sidestep guilt and shame inadequate? What *is* the only adequate response to our own sin?

6. Because of Adam's unique position as head of the original family and therefore captain of the whole human race, Adam's headship had particular significance for all of humanity. God dealt with him as a kind of legal delegate for himself, his wife, and all their offspring. When Adam sinned, he sinned as our representative before God. When he fell, we fell with him.

DISCUSS: What unique responsibilities are placed upon husbands and fathers? How might a wife help her husband fulfill his responsibilities before God? To what degree must a woman guard against blaming a husband for her own sin or the unrighteousness that might exist in her family?

7. Even in the wake of a curse, Eve could take hope in these four things: she was made subject to a husband who loved her rather than to the serpent to whom she had foolishly acquiesced; she remained Adam's partner and could still be his wife; she could still be the mother of all living; and, she had the hope that her Seed would one day bruise the Evil One's head.

DISCUSS: In the wake of consequences associated with your sin, what hope does the Lord hold out to you?

CHAPTER 2

1. Some of the words that might be used to describe Sarah are: impatient, temperamental, conniving, cantankerous, cruel, flighty, pouty, jealous, erratic, unreasonable, nag, manipulative. On the positive side, she is described in the Bible as having faith, great beauty, loyalty and love for her husband, being hospitable, having a sincere love for God, and having hope that never died.

DISCUSS: To what extent is every woman a "study in contrasts"—a mixture of negative and positive qualities? How important is it that we seek to overcome our negative traits and focus on our positive traits? To what extent can a pursuit of growing and developing positive traits lead to our overcoming negative traits? What difference does faith make in this growth-and-development process?

2. From what we read in Scripture, Sarah was not the least bit reluctant or unwilling to go with Abraham to a new place—even at retirement age.

DISCUSS: How difficult is it for some women to give up established homes, reputations, careers, family status, or community ties and move to new places? What makes that kind of life change something a woman embraces rather than opposes?

3. Sarah undoubtedly knew these three things with some degree of certainty: 1) her husband Abraham loved her and had a deep desire to protect her; 2) the Lord had placed a divine call on Abraham's life; and, 3) periodically, she and Abraham seemed to return to Bethel "to the place of the altar which he had made there at first. And there Abram called on the name of the LORD" (Gen. 13:4).

   DISCUSS: To what degree can a person deal with earthly inconvenience and challenging circumstances if she knows her husband loves her and will protect her in any way he can, her husband is pursuing what he believes fully to be God's plan for his life, and that worship and calling upon God are the touchstones to which her husband repeatedly returns?

4. Sarah sinned by suggesting that Abraham have a child by Hagar, and then by becoming angry and sending Hagar away to the desert to die. Abraham sinned by having sexual relations with Hagar and then refusing to mediate the differences between Sarah and Hagar. Hagar sinned by not protesting the relationship with Abraham and by becoming insolent to Sarah. The bitter fruit? Sarah remained childless for thirteen more years until Ishmael was "of age." Abraham eventually lost contact with his first-born son Ishmael. Hagar had a son who is described in Scripture as a "wild man" whose hands were "against every man and every man's hand against him" (Gen. 16:12).

   DISCUSS: In what ways do the consequences associated with sin generally remain even after God grants forgiveness?

5. Sarai means "my princess" and Sarah means "princess." Abram means "exalted father" and Abraham means "father of many nations." In removing the personal pronoun "my" from Sarah's name, the Lord was taking away any limiting aspect of her name. In changing Abram's name, the Lord was elevating him from a tribal leader to the founder of "many nations." In both cases, the "lid" was taken off the potential for both Sarah and Abraham.

   DISCUSS: What happens to a person's faith when that person begins to see that God has placed within him or her an unlimited potential?

CHAPTER 3

1. The term "extraordinary" is an understatement in describing how Rahab went from being a harlot in Jericho to being singled out for the greatness of her faith in Hebrews 11:31.

   DISCUSS: In what way or to what extent is the transformation of everyone who accepts Jesus Christ as personal Savior an "extraordinary" transformation?

2. Rahab and the Israelites who came to conquer the Amorites both had parents who were willfully disobedient to God and were thus subject to death. Neither Rahab's ancestors nor the ancestors of the conquering Israelites were deemed worthy to rule the Promised Land. Perhaps not our immediate parents or grandparents, but at some point in our family tree we all have ancestors who did not know Jesus.

   DISCUSS: "Divine grace redeemed [Rahab] and liberated her from all of that, plucking her as a brand from the fire". In what ways are we each plucked as a brand from the bonfire constructed by ancestors' sins?

3. Rahab knew that the Israelites were camped across the river, within walking distance of her city. She had no doubt heard about the Israelites' miraculous escape from Pharaoh and the drowning of the entire Egyptian army. The story of Israel's subsequent wanderings in the wilderness was also known. Rahab said to the spies, "As soon as we heard these things, our hearts melted; neither did there remain any more courage in anyone because of you."

   DISCUSS: In what ways does God prepare a person's heart to receive Jesus Christ as his or her Savior?

4. Rahab turned down an easy reward, put herself in jeopardy, and thus staked everything on the God of Israel. Nothing but faith could have made such a dramatic, instantaneous change in the character of such a woman.

   DISCUSS: What is the relationship between faith and boldness (or courage)?

5. Rahab asked the spies to spare her father, mother, brothers, sisters, and all that they had from death for the kindness she had shown them in sparing them from the king's henchmen. The spies said, "Our lives for yours, if none of you tell this business of ours." They also insisted that she bind a scarlet cord in the window of her home on the wall. They promised that whoever was in the house with her would be spared.

DISCUSS: What are the implications of Rahab's story for our trusting God to save all of our family members? How important is it to keep the promises that we make to one another?

6. To Rahab, the scarlet cord was a simple, expedient emblem suited to mark her window discreetly so that her house would be easily distinguishable from all the rest of the houses in Jericho. To Bible commentators, the scarlet color is reminiscent of the crimson sign of the blood sprinkled on the doorposts at the first Passover. Others see this scarlet cord as a deliberate symbol related to the shed blood of the ultimate Sacrificial Lamb, Jesus Christ.

DISCUSS: In what ways does the Lord sometimes ask His people to do things in very specific ways, even if they do not fully understand all of the meaning or symbolism of what they are doing? How important is it to obey God's methods *precisely*?

7. Rahab dealt with the Israelite spies in a very practical way, believing that their God was going to prevail over Jericho and that the Israelite God truly was and is "God in heaven above and on earth beneath" (Josh. 2:11). She hid the spies under flax on her roof; she let them down by a rope through the window of her home in the darkness of night; she gave them good advice about how to escape those who would pursue them. After they were gone, she insisted that her family members remain in her house with her.

DISCUSS: In what ways is faith "dead" without works? How do works keep faith alive? For whom and why is it important that we display our faith through works?

CHAPTER 4

1. Ruth was an outcast and an exile when she arrived in Israel, just as we each are outcasts and exiles as sinners before we come to know Jesus Christ as our Savior. Ruth had no hope of redeeming herself by any means. Her redemption was only possible through the grace of her mother-in-law's closest kinsman. In like manner, we cannot redeem ourselves. We must have Jesus as our Redeemer Kinsman.

   DISCUSS: Why is it important for us to remember that we can do nothing to save ourselves—our salvation is totally the work of Jesus Christ?

2. The Moabite religious practices typified everything abominable about idolatry—worship of the Moabite gods, especially Chemosh, involved human sacrifices, erotic imagery, and lewd conduct. Israelites and Moabites generally despised one another—their relationship ranged from uneasy tension to outright hostility. Marriage between Israelites and Moabites wasn't deemed appropriate.

   DISCUSS: How important are a common faith and cultural background to a marriage?

3. At the time Naomi made up her mind to return to Israel from Moab she was childless, widowed, impoverished, and aged, destitute of all land and possessions, and without any relatives close enough to count on them to care for her.

   DISCUSS: What more might be done in your community or church to identify and meet the needs of people who are poor and lonely?

4. Orpah wept with Naomi, kissed her mother-in-law, and returned to her family. Ruth wept with Naomi and clung to her, then voiced her firm resolve to stay with her.

   DISCUSS: What were the respective faith issues involved at this critical moment in the lives of Orpah, Ruth, and Naomi?

5. Boaz instructed Ruth to glean only in his fields and to stay close to his harvesters. He gave her permission to drink from the water he provided for his servants, instructed his young men not to touch her, and encouraged his workers to let grain fall purposely from their bundles for her sake. He spoke words of blessing to her. Boaz lightened the load of her labor and increased the reward of it.

   Ruth responded to Boaz by seeking his permission to glean from his fields, bowing before him, and working diligently in the fields until evening and then beating out the grain she had gathered. As a result of her work and the generosity shown to her by Boaz and his workers, she produced about four times as much grain for herself and Naomi as an average gleaner could hope to gather on a typical day.

   DISCUSS: How are these qualities of Boaz and Ruth indicative of what the Lord does for us?

6. A *goel* is a relative with the power or authority to initiate a rescue. A *goel* delivers or rescues a person who is in no position to rescue herself or himself.

   DISCUSS: What qualities make Jesus the one and only *Goel* for us?

7. Ruth "came softly, uncovered his feet, and lay down" by Boaz after the harvest feast was over and Boaz had fallen asleep. When Boaz awoke and asked her who she was she replied, "I am Ruth, your maidservant. Take your maidservant under your wing, for you are a *goel*." Ruth was borrowing language ("under your wing") from the blessing Boaz previously had given to her. This was, in effect, a marriage proposal.

   DISCUSS: In what ways do we sometimes err today by *not* being bold enough in asking the Lord for what we want? In what ways do we sometimes err today by being too presumptuous in assuming that the Lord must answer all of our requests in precisely the way and with the timing we desire? What is the tension between being humble and being bold—in having faith and yet not being presumptuous?

CHAPTER 5

1. Hannah was a woman whose life was crowned with grace, and who became a living emblem of the grace of motherhood.

DISCUSS: What is the meaning of the word "grace"?

2. Both Hannah and Sarah were the first wives of their husbands, both were childless and distraught over it, both were plagued with stress because of their husbands' bigamy (likely owing to their own barrenness), both ultimately received the blessing they sought from God, and both had sons who were prominent in the history of Israel.

   Both Hannah and Mary, the mother of Jesus, dedicated their firstborn sons to the Lord, were separated from their sons for critically important periods of time, and found that the surrender of their sons cost them dearly in terms of emotional suffering.

   Like both Mary and Sarah, Hannah was a woman of strong faith in Yahweh.

   DISCUSS: With which of these two women do you most closely identify and why?

3. Among the phrases used to describe Hannah's situation are: a devout family, living in a dismal period of Israel's history, regular trips to Shiloh to worship, troubled and sorrowful, her husband was a bigamist, no children, and tension in the family because Hannah's rival wife, Peninnah, deliberately provoked her.

   DISCUSS: What must life have been like for Hannah emotionally as the first but barren wife of Elkanah? (Keep in mind, also, that Hannah as the first wife was likely older than Peninnah.)

4. Hannah is described as having a love for her husband, a love for heaven, and a love for home.

   DISCUSS: How important is it for a woman to keep the "loves" of her life in right balance and priority?

5. Hannah did not pray for children, but for one son. She begged God for one son who would be fit to serve in the tabernacle. It wasn't about her. It wasn't about getting what she wanted. It was about self-sacrifice—giving herself to that little life in order to give him back to the Lord.

DISCUSS: What is the difference in being motivated to bear a child for your own self-fulfillment, self-gratification, or self-identity, and in seeking to bear a child in order to raise a godly servant of the Lord? How does the difference in motivation impact the way the mother relates to her child? How does the difference in motivation impact the child?

6. Hannah went to the Lord with her need and desire, not to her husband. Her frustration seems to have turned her more and more to the Lord, not away from Him. She persisted in prayer. She prayed with passion—with tears and travail.

   DISCUSS: How can we discern whether God's answer is "no" or "not yet"? What is the value of persisting in prayer?

7. Hannah's great prayer of thanksgiving and praise acknowledged God's holiness, goodness, sovereignty, power, and wisdom. Hannah worshiped Him as Savior, as Creator, and as sovereign Judge. In contrast, she acknowledged the fallenness and depravity of human nature, as well as the folly of unbelief and rebellion.

   DISCUSS: How important is it that our praise to God be based upon an intimate knowledge of Him?

8. Hannah continued to see Samuel during her visits to the tabernacle. She continued to give to him.

   DISCUSS: In what ways do mothers exert ongoing influence in their children's lives, even after their children are grown?

9. Hannah bore three sons and two daughters after she had given Samuel to the service of the Lord.

   DISCUSS: In what ways is the birth of every child an opportunity to love and serve the Lord? In what ways are we challenged to use the fruitfulness of our lives to tell others about the love and faithfulness of God?

CHAPTER 6

1. Note the words used to describe Mary: "most highly favored by God" and "most universally admired." To be blessed does not refer to a "saintly superhuman" state but to being sovereignly chosen by God and given remarkable grace and privilege. She is never depicted in Scripture as being a dispenser of grace, but rather the recipient of it.

   DISCUSS: In what ways do you feel blessed? In what ways are all followers of Christ Jesus blessed?

2. Mary should never be the object of religious veneration, imputed to having titles or attributes that belong to God alone. It is Jesus, not Mary, who is the fountain of grace. She must never be the central focus of worship or religious affection. Scripture makes no claim that she was untouched by original sin, a perpetual virgin, a co-redeemer with Christ, or the Queen of Heaven. She is not to be the object of prayers—God alone is omnipresent and omniscient and the One to whom we pray.

   DISCUSS: What is the correct Scriptural response to those who might be devoted to Mary or who make her an object of worship?

3. Mary is the equivalent of the Hebrew "Miriam," and the name means "bitter." Mary's young life may well have been filled with bitter hardships. Her hometown was a forlorn community in a poor district of Galilee, so good things probably were pretty scarce.

   She had a sister (John 19:25) and a close older relative named Elizabeth, the mother of John the Baptist (Luke 1:36), who might have been an aunt or a cousin. At the time the angel Gabriel appeared to her she was probably still a teenager. Girls in that culture were betrothed while they were as young as thirteen years of age. Mary was betrothed to Joseph, about whom we only know that he was a carpenter (Mark 6:3) and a righteous man (Matt. 1:19). She was a virgin (Luke 1:27).

   DISCUSS: Why are these attributes related to Mary important for us to consider when we study her life?

4. After briefly questioning Gabriel as to how she might conceive and bear a son as a virgin, Mary responded, "Behold the maidservant of the Lord! Let it be to me according to your word" (Luke 1:38). There's no evidence that Mary ever brooded over the effects her pregnancy would have on her reputation. She instantly, humbly, and joyfully submitted to God's will without further doubt or question.

DISCUSS: What often stands in the way of our instantly, humbly, and joyfully submitting to God's will without doubt or question?

5. Elizabeth's immediate response to Mary's voice gave Mary independent confirmation of what the angel had told her. Mary also felt free in Elizabeth's presence to voice her innermost praise to the Lord—an important confirmation of her own understanding about the child in her womb.

DISCUSS: How important is it to have confirmation about what the Lord speaks to us? How important is it to have an understanding about the true nature of God as we trust God to fulfill His promises and purpose in our lives?

6. Mary's song of praise is filled with joy, messianic hope, scriptural language, and references to the Abrahamic covenant.

DISCUSS: In what ways are we wise to incorporate these same qualities in our praise of the Lord?

7. Mary praised the Lord chiefly for His power, mercy, and holiness. She freely confessed God as the One who had done great things for her, and not vice versa. The song is all about *God's* greatness, *His* glory, the strength of *His* arm, and *His* faithfulness across the generations.

DISCUSS: How might we better keep our focus of praise on the nature and attributes of the Lord, rather than give in to the tendency to make our praise all about what the Lord has done to bless us personally?

8. Mary was present at the wedding at Cana, where Jesus performed His first miracle (John 2:1–5). She came to Him with other close family members out of concern for His safety and well-being (Mark 3:20–34). She was at the cross as Jesus was crucified (John 19:26–27).

DISCUSS: In what ways did these three incidents teach Mary how to submit to Jesus as her Lord, rather than try to control Him as His mother? How difficult is it for mothers to give up control over their grown children? How difficult is it for mothers to trust God to speak directly to their children, and to trust their children to hear directly from God?

CHAPTER 7

1. Those who recognized Christ at His birth included: Mary and Joseph; shepherds in the fields outside of Bethlehem, Simeon, and Anna. All of them recognized Him because they were told who He was by angels or by some other form of special revelation.

   DISCUSS: On what basis do we recognize Jesus as the Christ today?

2. Anna was a prophetess. She was the daughter of Phanuel, of the tribe of Asher. She was of great age. She had been a wife for seven years and had been a widow for many years. She did not leave the temple. She served God with fasting and prayer night and day. She thanked God for Jesus. She spoke of Jesus to all who looked for redemption in Jerusalem.

   DISCUSS: What parts of Anna's life description have special meaning to you?

3. Both Anna and Hannah were singled out for their practice of prayer and fasting. Both were perfectly at home in the temple. Both prophesied.

   DISCUSS: In what ways can every woman be like Anna and Hannah?

4. Anna was *unlike* Miriam in that her role as a prophetess did not seem to be an occasion for pride or rebellion. Anna was *unlike* Deborah in that there is no record of Anna ever giving advice as a "mother of Israel" to male leaders. Anna was *unlike* Huldah in that there is no record of Anna ever giving a Word of the Lord to priests or other spiritual leaders. Anna was *unlike* Noadiah, who is classified as a false prophet. Anna was *unlike* the wife of Isaiah, who seems to be called a prophetess only because of her association with her husband, a prophet. Anna was uniquely herself, proclaiming the Word of God to her fellow worshipers in the temple. In sum, Anna was *like* these women in being called a

"prophetess" but she did not fill the office of a prophet in the way that prophets such as Elijah or Jeremiah were prophets.

DISCUSS: What do you believe to be the role of "prophetesses" in the church today? (Base your answer upon what Scripture says!)

5. Anna was uniquely qualified to recognize baby Jesus as the Christ because she had been a faithful follower of the Lord for decades—quietly and faithfully serving the Lord in the temple, fasting and praying day and night. She had spiritual sensitivity and a strong faith. She was a mature believer.

DISCUSS: How does one become a mature Christian?

6. The Scripture says that Simeon pronounced his prophetic blessing on the infant Christ and His earthly parents, and in that instant Anna came along (Luke 2:38). Herod's temple was a massive structure. The encounter between Simeon and the parents of Jesus was unscheduled.

DISCUSS: Are there any coincidences for a Christian? What evidence have you seen in your own life that God is in control of all chance encounters?

CHAPTER 8

1. The well was Jacob's well, purchased so he could pitch his tent in the land of Canaan (Gen. 33:18–19). Jacob had also built an altar on the site. This location was the first inhabitable piece of real estate recorded in Scripture that any Israelite ever owned in the Promised Land. This was also the parcel of ground Jacob deeded to Joseph, and it was the place where Joseph's bones were finally interred. The burial of Joseph's remains at that location was a "significant reminder of God's faithfulness" (Acts 7:15–16). The deep well is spring-fed so the water is always fresh, pure, and cold. It is the only well—with the finest water—in an area where brackish springs abound. The existence of such a well on Jacob's property was deemed by the Israelites as a token of God's grace and goodness to their patriarch.

DISCUSS: How do the location of the story and the facts about the well itself add to the meaning of the story for you?

2. The Samaritans were considered unclean by the Israelites. The Samaritans were a mixed-race people descended from Assyrian pagans who had intermarried with Israelites. As early as the fifth-century BC, the Samaritans posed a serious threat to the purity of Israel. The Samaritans had blended Judaism with rank paganism, building a temple to rival the one in Jerusalem and developing a false priesthood.

   DISCUSS: Who or what ultimately determines if a person is pure?

3. Righteous Jewish men did not speak to unrighteous women. They did not drink from unclean vessels belonging to unclean people.

   DISCUSS: In what ways does Jesus ask us to defy human convention at times in order to tell other people about Christ and to share with them what He has done for us personally and what we believe He desires to be to us?

4. Jesus said that the water He gives satisfies completely so that a person need never be thirsty again. He also said that the water He gives becomes within a person "a fountain of water springing up into everlasting life" (John 4:13–14).

   DISCUSS: In what ways have you discovered this to be true in your life since you accepted Jesus as your Savior?

5. The Samaritan woman had been married five times and was presently living with a man who was not her husband. Jesus always confronts us with an awareness of our sin, even as He offers us forgiveness for sin.

   DISCUSS: Why is it important that we confess our sin to the Lord as a part of receiving Him as our Savior? In what ways is a confession of sin prior to forgiveness related to a confession after salvation that Jesus is a person's Savior and Lord?

6. Jesus said that true worshipers "worship the Father in spirit and truth" (John 4:23).

   DISCUSS: What does it mean to worship in spirit? In truth? What is our source of truth? How does God, who is Spirit, speak to a human being's spirit?

7. The Samaritan woman left her water pot at the well and went into the city to invite the leading men of the city to come out to the well to meet Christ. The person who has just had the burden of sin and guilt lifted always wants to share the good news with others. What was perhaps unusual was that she no longer evaded the fact of her sin or felt intimidated by the people of the city.

   DISCUSS: In what ways is forgiveness by the Lord both freeing and empowering?

8. Many of the Samaritans in Sychar "believed in Him"—and specifically "because of the word of this woman" (John 4:39). The Pharisees and scribes complained that Jesus conversed with rogues and scoundrels; they mocked Him for associating with sinners.

   DISCUSS: In what ways might we expect criticism when we spend time with sinners in order to tell them about Jesus Christ?

CHAPTER 9

1. Mary and Martha were *similar* in these ways: they both loved Jesus and cherished their friendships with Him, they both were profoundly influenced by Him, they both were beloved by Jesus. In addition, both of them were *similar* in their great love for their brother Lazarus; they both were profoundly distressed over his death. They were *dissimilar* in their personalities and the ways in which they expressed their devotion to Jesus.

   DISCUSS: How important is it for church members to focus on their similarities rather than on their differences?

2. Martha seems to be the elder sibling. Their home is described as Martha's house (Luke 10:38). Lazarus appears to be the youngest of the three, because he is named last in John's list of family members (John 11:5). They lived together in a home in Bethany, within easy walking distance of Jerusalem (about two miles southeast of the temple's eastern gate just over the Mount of Olives from Jerusalem's city center). We do not know how old they were when they developed their friendship with Jesus.

DISCUSS: How important is it for siblings to share a common faith and to serve the Lord together, in spite of personality differences and dissimilar talents or callings?

3. Mary's anointing of Jesus with costly oil is similar to an incident earlier in Jesus' ministry in which a repentant prostitute anointed Jesus' feet and wiped them with her hair. Jesus taught on that occasion: "Her sins, which are many, are forgiven, for she loved much" (Luke 7:47). Mary no doubt knew what had happened and what Jesus had said. She likely was seeking to show Jesus how much she loved Him. From Jesus' perspective, Mary was anointing Him for death and burial.

DISCUSS: Why do you believe Jesus allowed Mary to make such a lavish gesture toward Him?

4. The raising of their brother Lazarus ignited the plot among the Jewish leaders that finally ended with Jesus' death. When it came to Mary anointing Jesus with a costly outpouring of spikenard, Jesus' willingness to accept such a lavish expression of worship is what finally sealed Judas's decision to betray Christ.

DISCUSS: In what ways do our innocent acts of worship sometimes create intense anger or hatred in others? How common is it for hatred to have as its motivating factors either jealousy for power and status, or issues related to finances?

5. Mary sat at the feet of Jesus, listening to Him intently. Martha continued to work on preparations related to the meal. Each woman likely was being true to her own personality, and perhaps even to the characteristics often associated with first-born and second-born sisters.

DISCUSS: How important is it that we sometimes do what is out of character for us (personality-wise) in order to do what is most appropriate when it comes to serving and worshiping the Lord?

6. Martha ran from the house to meet Jesus. Mary remained in the house, immersed in grief (John 11:20). Martha seemed more concerned with the practicalities associated with her brother's death, burial, and gravesite. Mary

appeared to be more introspective and in deeper emotional anguish. Jesus dealt with each woman in distinctive and loving ways. He wept with Mary. He revealed to Martha that He is the Resurrection and the Life.

DISCUSS: How important is it to recognize that Jesus deals with us in ways that are geared specifically to our personalities and needs? How do we benefit from the sharing of our faith stories with other believers?

7. Martha was acting as if Christ needed her work for Him more than she needed His work on her behalf. Rather than humbly fixing her faith on the vital importance of Christ's work for sinners, she was thinking too much in terms of what she could do for Him. This seems to be the natural drift of the human heart. Human instinct seems to tell us that what we *do* is more important than what we believe.

DISCUSS: How might we better avoid the tendency to substitute good works for faith?

CHAPTER 10

1. Many people *incorrectly* believe that Mary Magdalene was the anonymous woman (identified only as a "sinner") in Luke 7:37–48, who anointed Jesus' feet and wiped them with her hair. But there is absolutely no reason to make that connection. Others *incorrectly* speculate that she was the woman described in John 8:1–12 as caught in the very act of adultery and saved from stoning by Christ. Long-discredited apocryphal stories about Mary Magdalene have recently been republished portraying Mary Magdalene as a mythical goddess figure, the writer of a gospel account, present at the Last Supper, and even the secret wife of Jesus and mother of earthly children by Him. *None* of these stories have scriptural or historical validity.

   Many Bible readers *correctly* know her as a woman delivered by Jesus from demonization, and as the first person to whom Christ revealed Himself after the resurrection.

DISCUSS: In what ways do media portrayals and historical myths sometimes give us a false impression about Bible people, and thus a false understanding of Scripture?

2. Demonic possession is associated with a number of symptoms in the New Testament: insanity, physical infirmities (including blindness, deafness, an inability to speak, fits and seizures, and general infirmity), and other examples of "bondage to an evil spirit." Scripture *does* make a clear distinction between demon possession and diseases, including epilepsy and paralysis (Matt. 4:24). Demon possession involves bondage to an evil spirit—a real, personal, fallen spirit-creature—that indwells the afflicted individual. Scripture portrays demon possession as an affliction, not a sin per se. Some of the descriptive terms that might be associated with the demonically possessed in the Scripture include: tormented, miserable, sorrowful, lonely, heartsick, forlorn, pitiable, outcast, pariah, victim, restless, hopeless, friendless, joyless, in agony, morose, tortured, demented.

   DISCUSS: What is the error of assuming that demons do *not* exist or that demonic possession is *not* real? How should demonically possessed people be "treated" today?

3. Some demon-possessed people were brought to Jesus (Matt. 8:16, 9:32; Mark 9:20), sometimes He called them to Himself or went to them (Luke 13:12 and Matt. 8:28–29), and sometimes demons were already present upon His arrival.
   Demons cried against Jesus (Luke 4:34) and sometimes caused violent convulsions (Mark 9:20) to get the wretched person away from Christ.

   DISCUSS: What is our responsibility in bringing demon-possessed people to Christ for deliverance? How do we do that today?

4. Mary Magdalene is listed by name as one of the women who accompanied Jesus as He "went through every city and village, preaching and bringing the glad tidings of the kingdom of God" (Luke 8:1).

   DISCUSS: Why was Mary Magdalene in a unique position of having nothing to lose and nothing to prove in leaving behind everything else and following Jesus in His ministry? In what ways are we to "accompany" Jesus today?

5. Although Jesus was criticized for many things by His enemies, He was never criticized for the way He treated the women who were His disciples or for any unseemliness or indiscretion in the way He treated the women as a whole.

DISCUSS: Why is it important that *every* person in ministry treat those who are close followers of their teaching and preaching with the utmost purity, respect, and discretion?

6. Mary is apparently the only one of the close circle of Jesus' disciples who did all of the following: heard Jesus speak from the cross (John 19:25–27), knew from personal observation where Jesus had been buried (Mark 15:47), went to the tomb with burial spices on the first day of the week (Luke 23:55–56 and Mark 16:1), saw the empty tomb (Mark 16:5 and Luke 24:3), saw angels in the tomb and heard the angel's proclamation (John 20:12; Matt. 28:6; Mark 16:6; Luke 24:6), and encountered Jesus in the garden after all others had left (John 20:15–17).

   DISCUSS: What does Mary Magdalene's example teach us about devoted love and faithfulness?

CHAPTER 11

1. Lydia was the original convert for the gospel in Europe, the first person on record to respond to the message of Christ during Paul's original journey into Europe. Irony? Lydia was not European. She was most likely from the region of Lydia, a large Asian province known for its capital, Sardis, and its most famous ruler, Croesus, who captured the wealth of the Medo-Persian Empire and used it to conquer most of the known world. In many ways, Lydia's conversion was the toehold that conquered Europe for the gospel.

   Lydia was originally from Thyatira, known for having one of the seven churches mentioned in the book of Revelation. She was a businesswoman engaged in the textile industry.

   DISCUSS: What influence can just one seemingly insignificant and unlikely person have in God's plan and purpose?

2. God had led Paul and his missionary team into Europe by means of a dream in which a Macedonian man "stood and pleaded with [Paul], saying, 'Come over to Macedonia and help us'" (Acts 16:9). Lydia was among the first people Paul met once he arrived in Macedonia and its foremost city, Philippi. Rather than reach Lydia in the region she regarded as home, the gospel pursued her to Europe.

DISCUSS: In what ways is each person's "salvation story" the most amazing and important miracle of his or her life?

3. Lydia already was an active seeker of God. She had aligned herself with a group of devout Jewish women. She was meeting for prayer. She listened with rapt attention and understanding as Paul and his companions explained the gospel message. Her heart was truly open.

   DISCUSS: In what ways do we need to be more like Lydia, even if we have known Jesus as our Savior and Lord for many years?

4. Don't imagine for a moment that there is any kind of violent force or coercion involved when God draws people to Christ. Grace doesn't push sinners against their wills toward Christ; it draws them willingly to Him—by first opening their hearts. It enables them to see their sin for what it is and empowers them to despise what they formerly loved. It also equips them to see Christ for who He truly is. Someone whose heart has been opened like that will inevitably find Christ Himself irresistible. The Lord simply opened Lydia's heart to believe—and she did.

   DISCUSS: Why is it essential that we open our hearts to the possibility that Jesus is the Savior? What is it essential that we allow ourselves, or choose, to believe? What happens if a person closes his or her heart to the possibility that Jesus is the Savior or actively refuses to believe?

CHAPTER 12

1. Reflect on these moral qualities or spiritual traits in the following twelve women we've studied:

   Eve: perseverance in faith and expectation

   Sarah: steadfast hope that persevered against unbelievable obstacles

   Rahab: God's grace can rebuild a sin-ravaged life

   Ruth: devotion, love, trust, humility

Hannah: dedication of motherhood, making one's home a place where God is honored above all

Mary, the mother of Jesus: humble submission

Anna: faith witness to the grace and glory of God

Samaritan woman: eager response to the gospel message

Martha and Mary: twin virtues of worship and service, prompted by deep devotion to Christ

Mary Magdalene: Christ's deliverance and forgiveness prompting great love

Lydia: a heart that was wide open to Christ

DISCUSS: What do you believe would be the foremost moral quality or spiritual trait that someone might use to describe you and your relationship to the Lord?

2. Bible women play prominent roles in many key biblical narratives. Wives are seen as venerated partners and cherished companions to their husbands, not merely slaves or pieces of household furniture (Gen. 2:29–24; Prov. 19:14; Eccl. 9:9), and God commanded children to honor *both* father and mother.

DISCUSS: How have women played prominent roles in the "church narratives" associated with your life, and in the history and collective life of the church you attend?

3. They partook with men in all the feasts and public worship of Israel (Deut. 16:14; Neh. 8:2–33). Women were not required to be veiled or silent in the public square (Gen. 12:14; 24:16; 1 Sam. 1:12). Mothers (not merely fathers) shared teaching responsibilities and authority over their children (Prov. 1:8, 6:20). Women could even be landowners in Israel (Num. 27:8; Prov. 31:16). In fact, wives were expected to administer many of the affairs of their own households (Prov. 14:1; 1 Tim. 5:9–10, 14).

These roles for women in Israel were different from the roles for women in most of the ancient cultures and in the Roman Empire. Pagan religion tended to fuel and encourage the devaluation of women even more. Women in the early church were present with the chief disciples on the day of Pentecost. Some were renowned for their good deeds, hospitality, or understanding of sound doctrine and spiritual giftedness (Acts 1:13–13, 16:14–15, and 18:26).

DISCUSS: In what ways does modern culture denigrate women? In what ways is the church to be an example to the world in the way it treats women?

4. Jesus encouraged the discipleship of women, revealed His identity as the Christ to women, blessed their children, healed them, restored them to their families and communities, raised their dead, forgave their sin, and restored their virtue and honor. He always treated women with the utmost dignity. (Refer to Mark 9:20–22; Luke 7:37–50; John 4:7–27.)

DISCUSS: In what ways and on what basis can women today trust Jesus to do for them what He did for women during His earthly ministry?

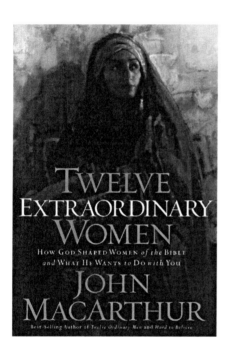

THE MACARTHUR
SCRIPTURE MEMORY SYSTEM

JOHN MACARTHUR POURS HIS HEART into his work as a Bible teacher, and now he teaches Scripture, literally one verse at a time, with *The MacArthur Scripture Memory System.* The System comes in a turned-edge book, complete with the following timeless elements:

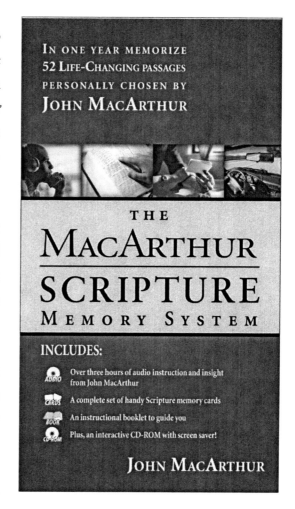

- 3 audio CDs with Dr. MacArthur reading the verse-of-the-week, and providing a brief statement of what that verse means and why it is so important to remember.

- A handy pack of printed cards, one for each verse, so that you can put one in your wallet or purse to refresh your memory of the weekly verse.

- CD-ROM containing a dynamic desktop complete with the text of each week's verse and a link to listen to the audio of the verse! Also contains a screen saver with each week's verse.

ISBN: 0-7852-5061-1

For old and new Bible readers alike, *The MacArthur Scripture Memory System* is an excellent way to really get into the Word and commit it to memory.

THOMAS NELSON
Since 1798

For other products and live events,
visit us at: **thomasnelson.com**

CPSIA information can be obtained at www.ICGtesting.com
Printed in the USA
LVOW09s0428070214

372744LV00002B/4/P

9 781418 505578